Dr. T's Living Well S

SENIOR MOMENTS

A Guide for Aging Safely and Gracefully.

By Dr. Richard L. Travis

Thank You *for purchasing this book.*

"Senior Moments: A Guide for Aging Safely and Gracefully"

First Printing: 2020
Print Edition

RLT Publishing
www.rltpublishing.com

Please Visit: **www.drrichardtravis.com/**

Introduction

If you are over 65 years old, you are considered a "senior." (Unfortunately, some organizations and businesses label you as a senior even as early as 50 years old.) Well if being called a senior comes with a few benefits, like a business deciding to give you a discount --- take it. One of my friends calls the 65th birthday the Red, White, and Blue birthday—to identify the colors of Medicare. I will refer to those of us over 65 years of age as seniors in this guide. Other words that could be used would be the wise ones, mature, seasoned, baby boomers, elders, and probably many more...

This book is a book about how to make getting older a little easier.

I have looked at the different aspects of our daily life and pondered what would make things go smoother, and what assistance could we use to benefit us as we age.

So, I have embarked on making a guidebook of sorts giving you many suggestions, which may or may not apply to you, based on your gender, your age, your health, and your financial situation.

At the end of the book is a complex list of videos from YouTube, articles, or references to compare costs, and reviews of some of the items discussed in this book. If you are using an internet-linked device to read this book, then each of the items in the Reference section are Hyperlinked or clickable for you to go right to that reference and read about it.

Please feel free to write me at drrichardtravis@gmail.com if you have found that I left something out that you think could be included.

I have discovered in my many years as a Psychotherapist that we do not learn anything new unless we want to learn, and we are ready to learn. Enjoy!

Dedication

I never really thought about living to be 73 years old, but here I am. Not only have I survived, I am comparatively healthy and happy. I do notice, however, several people around my age, who have different levels of health issues and impairments.

This observation has led me to do some research into what would make an older person's life a little easier. Of course, we would all benefit from a full-time maid or cook, but for most of us that is not realistic.

So, this book is dedicated to the middle class, and the working class of people who are not millionaires, or able to easily move to an expensive assisted living facility. If you gain one thing from this book that makes your life safer and easier as you age, then I have accomplished my mission. If you gain many things from this book that make your life simpler and easier, then I am incredibly grateful to have been the one to enlighten you.

Table of Contents

YOUR HEALTH

We all know that our health is the most important thing in our life. If you are healthy, do everything you can do to stay that way. If you have health challenges, do everything you can do to get better and live the highest quality of life you can. Here some general hints about keeping healthy.

HINT: Choose your doctors carefully:

This is a time in your life when checkups are crucial. Even Medicare mandates an annual checkup to those of us over 65 years old. Choose your Primary Care Physician carefully. You want someone who will listen and who knows what a senior might be experiencing. In general, men probably ought to see a male physician and females a female physician. Some might disagree with me on this, but we need to be able to talk about and show everything to our physician with as little discomfort as possible. We need to feel emotionally safe in our physician's office.

I love to hear the names of the physicians who other people use, and I also love to go to the physician's website and look at their reviews. There are reviews posted everywhere today, so look them up to help make good choices.

Specialists that many of us seniors start seeing are cardiologists, dermatologists, endocrinologists, podiatrists, ophthalmologists, and ear, nose, and throat specialists to name a few. Please do reviews online about someone you may go see.

I recently recommended someone to see a female psychiatrist who was new in town. My friend looked her up online and said the reviews were terrible and found another psychiatrist nearby who had amazing reviews. She was happy with her choice. Please do not count on your family or Primary Physician to know who the best specialist would be for you. Of course, many of us are restricted by our insurance, but still be vigilant about your research online about that physician.

I had been going to the "best" ophthalmologist in town until recently. In this current "interesting" political climate, he started lecturing me about certain Senators and bills being discussed in Congress. I was totally his captive as he was examining my eyes, so I said nothing. He assumed I was in the sphere of his political belief system for whatever reason, and I was not. I felt so badly for all the other older folks in that waiting room who would be subjected to his political tirades on that day. I set up my next annual appointment with a lovely female physician in the same office and have been incredibly happy with her. *Physicians should not mix politics with medicine!*

You, or a loved one, may unfortunately have a genetic predisposition for certain diseases such as diabetes, or cancer. There are also many other possible difficult health challenges we all might face, like Alzheimer's, or Dementia, or serious vision problems. Be vigilant about your health and your doctor's visits. Do not allow a physician to pat you on the head or the shoulder and send you off without the information and referrals that you need. We need to be assertive about our own healthcare.

HINT: Write a list of things you want to discuss with your doctor:

Take some time the day before a doctor's visit, especially before your annual visit with your Primary Physician, to write a list of things you wish to discuss. When you first walk into the exam room let the doctor know that after the exam you a have short list of things to go over. Most of us walk away from our doctor's visit wishing we would have discussed something additional.

HINT: Pick Health Insurance that Works for you:

I am not an insurance salesman or an expert on health insurance, but I do know a few things about those of us 65 and older. Every fall you can change your Medicare insurance selection for the upcoming calendar year. Factors that probably affect your choice would be your financial situation, your health conditions, physician availability, plans available, and the area in which you live.

As far as I understand, you can choose: 1. Medicare only and pay the additional 20% of charges from the physician or hospital; or you can choose: 2. Medicare and pay for a Secondary and a prescription plan; or you can choose: 3. Medicare HMO at a very low monthly cost; or you can choose: 4. Medicare Advantage Plan. I will have several links at the end of the book for you to get more details on these choices. Each has different costs and different benefits.

I highly recommend finding a local Medicare-knowledgeable agent who will sit with you, with no expectations you will buy his plan, and go over the options with you. Some areas have seminars at community centers going over this. Look at all your options. *I have included several articles and videos at the end of this guide for you to gather more exacting information about Medicare and Medicaid. Link: (Social Security, Medicare Benefits: https://www.ssa.gov/benefits/medicare/)*

HINT: Men should go to the Physician:

I have read that men are much more reluctant to go to the doctor than women. Is that why they have a shorter life span? There are so many insurance choices for seniors today. Choose one that is affordable and go for checkups. Yes, it is embarrassing to discuss some things, but do you know what women have had to go through their whole lives at doctors' offices?

HINT: Women do not forget your annual (at least) Gynecological exam:

We pick on men for not going to the doctor enough, but women need to remember to have their OBGYN exams yearly, until told otherwise.

HINT: Do not talk endlessly to others about your doctor visits:

Unless you have a special friend or spouse with whom you can exchange doctor stories, try not to take up all social discussions with others by discussing your health issues, or doctor visits. Find other more current things to discuss. I have a friend who has established a rule among his friends when they gather for dinner: The first 20 minutes is for the "organ recital," and then no more health issue discussion for the evening. Works for me.

HINT: Find a support group:

If you do have serious or chronic health issues, please do not isolate. Find a support group. If one is not near you, find one online. Never suffer alone.

HINT: Exercise:

If possible, exercise. Most Medicare plans offer free gym memberships. Go, even if to only walk on the treadmill. Some of you may not be able to exercise, or go to the gym, but do what you can to keep your circulation moving.

When you go to the grocery store, park farther from the entrance than you need to get in extra steps. Make sure you wear good walking shoes when you are walking. Take dance classes if you can. Take exercise classes at the gym. Walk your dog more often. During inclement weather, walk around inside the nearest mall. Finding a friend to walk with is also a great motivator to getting those comfortable shoes on and chatting about life while walking around the neighborhood.

HINT: Make sure you have properly fitted shoes for walking:

Bad shoes not only hurt your toes, feet and back, but they can be a trip hazard as you walk.

If your knee or hip are interfering with your ability to walk, please be more aggressive about getting medical advice on them. Yes, sometimes it may require surgery, but read about the many successes, and consider how much freedom you will have with improved movement. Surgery should always be the last choice. Look into the latest natural product: CBD oil. Many people are finding great relief from joint pain by taking CBD oil twice a day. Do your research!

Motivate yourself by purchasing a device to wear on your wrist that monitors steps, miles walked, stairs climbed daily, weekly, and monthly. It is quite motivating to watch the number of steps taken each day increase on your Fitbit, or Apple Watch.

HINT: At the very least—Stretch:

There is a great deal written about how important it is to move our arms and wrists and neck. We need to stretch to keep the blood flowing through our joints, keeping them lubricated and healthy. Even stretching from a sitting position has tremendous benefits.

FOOD AND EATING

As we age, many of us tire of cooking and go out to dinner or lunch more often. Even though we might be eating less as we age, by going out to dinner so much we often eat food that is either not necessarily the best for us, or it is too fattening. Make wise choices when going out to eat.

<u>HINT: Many restaurants have daily or weekly specials:</u>

It's fun to find the local restaurants that have specials on different days of the week. These specials usually cut down on the cost of going out to eat. Even Groupon (Groupon: https://www.groupon.com/) offers discounts on various restaurants. Two days of the week we go to places that offer such good prices on dinner, that we go there and get to bring leftovers home for another meal.

<u>HINT: Find APPS to download on your phone to get special deals at fast casual food chains:</u>

One thing you might consider doing is seeing if your favorite fast-casual restaurants might have apps that you can download to your smart phone. Boston Market for example sends out BOGO (buy one, get one) specials to my smart phone at least twice a month. (https://apps.apple.com/us/app/boston-market/id373559901) There are many other apps for food and restaurants in the Resource section of this guide book.

<u>HINT: You can have food delivered that you can cook:</u>

There have been several companies popping up lately that will deliver pre-packaged food to you for lunch and dinner that require minimal preparation. The box may contain all the ingredients for you to make a chicken dinner, for example. You just follow the directions and cook it. These services are not inexpensive but made for those who want a simpler dinner preparation and do not want to go shopping for groceries.

There are some companies listed in the Resource section in the back of the book.

HINT: Many restaurants offer AARP or Senior Citizen Discounts:

Again, with a little research online you may find places to eat which offer discounts to seniors. It may only be on special days, but a discount is a discount. Olive Garden, Applebee's, Red Lobster, and Cracker Barrel are all possible places for special pricing for seniors, or they may offer discounts when you sign up online to their website.

HINT: You can have your groceries delivered by Costco and many local grocery stores.

Are you feeling too tired to go grocery shopping, or healing from some surgery? Look online to see who delivers groceries. Walmart, Costco, BJ's, and Publix near me deliver groceries for a small fee. Even Amazon can deliver many grocery items. I would recommend that you go to the grocery store if you are able, so that you can get the exercise and socialization that is so important for our physical and mental health.

SEX

Yes, Sex! There is no rule written anywhere that after 65 years of age we should not have sex. We just probably should not talk about it too much. We do not want to shock the "young-uns." If you are healthy and continue to take care of your body, there is no reason why you should not have a healthy sex life. Of course, it is always nice to have a good partner, spouse, mate, friend with whom to have sex.

HINT: Don't Give up having Sex:

Many years ago, I met a wonderful, wise woman in her early 90's who had read an article about me in the local newspaper doing hypnosis. She wanted to learn self-hypnosis to use at the dentist's office. She was an excellent student and ended up teaching many others to do self-hypnosis. During our sessions I learned a great deal about her life and about her life with her now deceased husband. One day she leaned over to me quite intimately and said, "Dr. Travis, is it okay if I have sex?" She was deeply religious and I asked her if she had asked her priest. She said, "What would he know?" I laughed and told her that it was my belief that if you are not hurting anyone, God gave us that body to use and enjoy. She sighed and smiled, and said, "I am so relieved you didn't judge me." Judge her? I thought it was incredible that she was still having orgasms at 93 years old. She leaned in again to admit she had no partner, and did I still think that was okay. I smiled and said, "You would make a lot of women over 65 years old jealous, if they knew one of the reasons why you are so constantly satisfied with life."

Men tend to have erection problems as they age, due to medications, or health or weight, or alcohol issues. There is a great deal of help with that problem today. Cialis, Viagra, Levitra, Spedra, and Staxyn are all medications that could help. Just please go to a urologist if your erections disappear. You should be capable of having a healthy sex life years and years into your retirement.

HINT: If you are single and having sex with others, be Safe:

Sexually Transmitted Diseases (STDs) and HIV are not exclusively for younger folks. In fact, there is a large increase in STDs and HIV transmission among the population over 65. So, protect yourself, and be safe. If you are sexually active and single, make sure your Primary Care Physician is aware, so that you can get the appropriate blood work done with your regular blood work.

HEARING

I believe that all insurance plans offer visits to an audiologist.

If you think others are mumbling all the time, or you must turn up the television often, you probably need to have your hearing checked. It is natural to have some hearing loss as we age. Our hearing loss makes us miss out on conversations and makes others suffer. People with hearing loss often talk louder and ask to have things repeated a great many times.

HINT: Investigate Sound Bars for your Television:

You can now purchase special soundbars that you hook up to your television that help you hear the voices and improve the quality of the music. There are specific sound bars which are known to improve the quality of the voices, for those of us who might have difficulty understanding the voices through the music and other sound effects. They are seriously worth the money, especially if you have a flat screen television with the small speakers. Do your research online and ask friends what they use. I bought the most recommended brand, and then listened to a friend's sound bar. The difference was like night and day. I returned mine and bought one of his brand (Yamaha) through Amazon.

Please read the resource section on Sound Bars at the end of this guide to learn how to hook up sound bars and which ones do what to the sound.

HINT: Is it Time for Hearing Aids:

If it is recommended that you get hearing aids, do not quickly buy the model that the audiologist is selling. There is a great range in prices and quality of hearing aids. If you need them, get them. But do your research online. You may even have an insurance plan that pays for part of the cost. It is also worth the cost of a membership to look at Costco for what they offer. They are usually half the price for the best model.

Hearing aids are not inexpensive. But it is often true that you get what you pay for. You may want to try the inexpensive hearing aids advertised in magazines and the newspapers but try to make sure they have a money back guarantee. Most of the inexpensive hearing aids only enhance the sound, but do not have the many great features of hearing aids recommended by professionals.

VISION

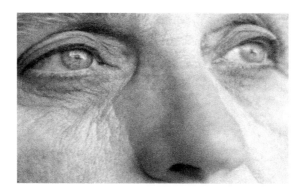

Another concern as we age is that of declining or impaired vision. Be vigilant about going to your ophthalmologist at least once a year. If your vision changes between visits, make an appointment. Do not wait. You are not bothering them. This is their job. Sometimes, you might just need your glasses adjusted. Read about what may occur to your eyes or your vision as you age, so you can be more prepared.

Wear sunglasses to protect your eyes outside. Read about the vegetables to eat which are good for vision. Some people swear by supplements that they take for vision care.

HINT: Night Lights are a Necessity:

A great investment to have is a bathroom nightlight. You also might have two or three nightlights placed strategically around the house. They are very inexpensive and could prevent a bump or a fall. You can find them at the dollar store for only one dollar. There are many styles from which to choose.

HINT: Get Timers for your lights:

A trip to the hardware store, Home Depot or Lowes and you could bring home a couple of timers to plug your lamps into in different rooms. They can be programmed to come on at dusk and go off at your bedtime. I find them to be extremely helpful.

HINT: Driving after dark:

Some people feel the only thing that changes with their vision as they have aged is difficulty seeing at night. Please be careful about driving after dark if you are one of those people. You can always use Uber or Lyft or a taxi if you must go out in the evening. Or find someone who has excellent night vision to be the driver.

A friend told me that she noticed that it was getting harder to see well in dimly lit areas. She found that she was having trouble distinguishing between navy and black clothing in her closet. Eventually she was diagnosed with cataracts. As the cataracts worsened, so did her vision in poor lighting. She found a way to compensate by hanging black items on black hangers and navy items on green hangers (...because those were the most accessible colors in her stores). This little 'trick' has helped her immensely!

SLEEPING

Our sleeping habits change over time. Some of us are more sedentary in the daytime as we age, so sleep does not come easily. Sleeping straight through the night is difficult. Also, many of us find the need to get up at night to use the bathroom.

Good sleep is important. It is important for your physical and your mental health. Make sure your bed is comfortable, and even the pillow is right for you. Many people even find putting a small pillow between their knees is helpful for a good night's sleep. Also, the temperature of the bedroom should be appropriate for your needs.

HINT: Clearing the Mind Before bedtime:

It does not matter how much money you have, how healthy you are, or even how fortunate you feel your life is—there are always things to worry about. It is important however that these worries do not interfere with sleep. Before you turn off the lights and slide under the covers, take a moment or two to clear your mind. Start by sitting on the edge of your bed and taking a few nice deep breaths. Breath out the worries, the thoughts left over from the day, the problems not solved yet, the tasks yet to do. If you need to, imagine a file cabinet, and visualize each item floating around your brain right now being placed into a file which you will access tomorrow upon awakening. Close the file drawers and lie down and go to sleep.

HINT: Does Pain keep you Awake?

Make sure your physician knows if pain keeps you awake or awakens you at night. There are many over the counter herbal remedies to try first or Aleve, Motrin, or similar pain relievers. There are also prescriptions which your doctor might suggest.

Some people are turning to CBD oil and its anti-inflammatory properties to help alleviate pain. Do your research, as there are many CBD distillers in the marketplace including online. You would want to try one that has no THC in it. So, the purer the CBD oil is, the better. Again, research is essential. The amount of CBD in a product will be noted in mg (milligrams) while the amount of oil with which it is mixed is noted in ml (milliliters). There are also CBD creams and lotions with CBD.

My chiropractor introduced me to CBD oil after he saw how it helped his 76-year-old father. His father is not only sleeping better because of pain reduction, but is golfing again, after stopping for years due to joint pain.

HINT: Try Sleeping Aids:

There are many medications your physician can prescribe you to improve your sleep but go to the health food store first and try herbal products. Herbal products do not tend to have mind-altering effects as most prescriptions do. Check out the Homeopathic section of Whole Foods to see what items they must help you sleep. It is worth a try.

Prescription sleep aids are an option of course, but a big concern is that if you need to use the bathroom at night will your head be clear enough for you to walk and not hurt yourself on the way to the bathroom? Addiction to sleep medications is also a concern, as some medications have long-term effects on the brain. If you are in a state where medical marijuana is legal, there is a CBD product that has a small amount of THC in it and can be quite helpful for sleep. You may need to get a license from a physician to purchase this type of CBD product. You can read more about CBD and the reviews at the end of this book.

SENSE OF SMELL

Another change that most of us do not expect is that our sense of smell changes. Most of us, as we age, do not have the same keen sense of smell as we did in earlier years. This becomes problematic when it comes to odors in your home, or on your clothing, or in your car, or perhaps even in cooking.

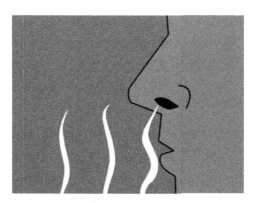

HINT: Go Lightly on Cologne and Perfume:

Have you ever been in a restaurant or theatre when someone was seated near you and then they either moved or asked to be moved? Chances are your cologne or perfume may have been too strong. Try just putting on a little dab behind the ears ladies and gentlemen. We are not trying to fill the room with the scent of our favorite smell. I have a friend who says, "I feel like I just stepped into a perfume bottle," when someone passes by who has "overdone" it.

We want a gentle aroma that is pleasant around us. So, when people walk by or sit near us, they really do not get hit with a sledgehammer of cologne or perfume, but people might get a pleasant scent if they are physically close. My thought is that if I can smell your perfume or cologne before I hug you then it is probably too big of a dose that you used.

I go early to the theatre to get a good seat for the movie. I get so frustrated when some people come and sit in front of us or behind us, and one of them was doused in perfume or cologne. We must move to less desirable seats, or I will have sneezing fits. (It is not just seniors who overdo perfumes and colognes, but if the shoe fits....)

HINT: Air out the Moth Balled clothing:

I was at dinner the other night when a lovely couple came and sat near us. We were already eating, but something smelled strange. I finally figured out that the woman had probably stored her jacket in mothballs and took it out to go to dinner. It was a horrific experience for us, but what can you say? She probably has no idea that it reeked of mothballs.

Supposedly our sense of smell adjusts in 20 minutes, or so I have read. But I have never adjusted to that moth ball smell. No wonder people put mothballs out around the outside of their house to keep cats from using their garden as a litter box. Moth balls are very unpleasant.

HINT: Bathe daily:

As mentioned before, our sense of smell deteriorates somewhat as we age. One thing that is extremely important to do is to make sure our body is clean. Shower or bathe daily. Do not just do a once over with a washcloth. Bathe your entire body, ensuring you eliminate not only odors but odor causing bacteria that you may have accumulated that day. I remember hearing stories of grandchildren going back to their mother after a visit with their grandparents saying, "mom, Grandpa stinks." Do not use cologne or perfume as a coverup and an excuse not to bathe your entire body.

YOUR MIND

We also need to pay attention to keeping our minds as healthy as possible. Yes, as we age, we do have memory changes. We do often forget why we walked into this room, or where we put the keys. Busy people in their thirties, forties and fifties also misplace keys, or forget why they walked into a room because their mind was busy. So, first, do not punish yourself if you cannot remember the name of that movie, or the word you wanted to say. It happens to most of us. Second, let us do something to slow down the mental aging process.

HINT: Stop Drinking Alcohol:

There are many studies of how alcohol negatively affects our brain. Our brain ages quicker from overuse of alcohol. A glass of wine a day may not be harmful, but I hope you will read why I say <u>overuse </u>of alcohol is a contributor to early onset dementia, and forgetfulness.

Alcohol use in seniors also effects balance and coordination. If you want to see seniors who overdrink, go on a cruise, and watch some of the seventy-somethings wobble into the dining room, drink in hand talking loudly and laughing even louder. While they certainly are entitled to those drinks, my concern is the long-term effects on their brains and organs (to say nothing of the people who may have to suffer listening to them.)

HINT: Challenge your Brain:

Many folks after retirement do little to stimulate their brains other than solving the puzzle on Wheel of Fortune. So, challenge your brain -- Read a book. Do word puzzles. Write a book. Learn a new language. Start a new hobby. Join a book club. Research new recipes for healthy foods you have wanted to try. Build a birdhouse. Start growing plants, or flowers.

Most public libraries offer books to lend, but now they lend them electronically as well. You can also download the Kindle app on any kind of tablet, laptop or computer and purchase online books, or borrow them from the library. Audio books also challenge the mind and are available from the library, on Amazon and elsewhere.

Start gathering those old photos and put together some photo albums to give to relatives. Take a neighbor or friend to the movie theatre to see a movie you would not normally see. Going to the movie theatre in the afternoon is nice, as fewer people are there to deal with.

Watch more documentaries on television. A new streaming service called Curiosity Streaming has so many great informative series to amaze you and your senses. Netflix streaming has an entire category of documentaries. We are never too old to learn. But we can be too lazy or not proactive enough.

YOUR PERSONALITY

Your personality is affected by sleep, illness, finances, legal issues, family issues, grief and among other things—age. You may be someone who feels that your personality is fixed as it is, but you must have seen people who have changed, good or bad, after retirement. People are easily affected by the environment, and when you are no longer the "boss" or the "worker bee" or the active mother or father, you change a little.

HINT: Nobody wants to be around a "Know-it-All":

I have asked many seniors what personalities they see in other seniors. It is amazing how many people tell me that some older folks become "know-it-alls." This is the person who has an answer for everything, even when not asked. He or she will interrupt to offer an opinion, which usually comes across as a fact. Do not dare dispute this "know-it-all" as you will be over talked, or belittled, or even have a voice raised at you. Also do not ask where the "know-it-all" got information, because that is not something that is important for the "know-it-all" to cite.

I am told that many "know-it-alls" are spouting conspiracy theories as they try to get everyone's attention and admiration. Sadly, "know-it-alls" do not get positive attention, but most often the cold shoulder, or avoidance by others.

HINT: Nobody wants to be around a Cranky Person or a Whiner:

I realize that the word cranky is an old-fashioned word that is not used much any-more. But if you are reading this then you probably know what that word means. We have many examples of people in our lives that have had surgeries, divorces, financial hits, family problems, or other losses. How you respond to those crises show us your personality.

If you are constantly complaining, or bemoaning your misery, people will start avoiding you. I am not saying you aren't entitled to feel sorry for yourself, and even complain a little to close friends. That is natural. The problem is when your whining or crankiness becomes who you are. Life is no longer having any joyous moments for you, and you live in your misery. Do everything in your power to get out of that crankiness or whining as soon as you can. You run the risk of chasing away everyone dear to you, even family.

I have an acquaintance that is in her late 70's. She has a meager income but lives well enough. She has had some losses and traumas in her life, even estrangement from a daughter. She has blended into some wonderful people in recent years that love her and take care of her. The problem is that as she has aged, she has lost all filters as to what she should or could say. These loving friends of hers tell me that she comes to their house and lectures them on politics and religion. She seems to not know how to stop her opinionated rants and raves and has no clue she is insulting others.

If you are one of those people, you might need to seek counseling to interrupt this negative nature if it continues. Hopefully, someone dear to you will take your hand and sit you down and tell you how your personality has changed, and it has become toxic to most people. Hopefully, you will not be offended, but take that as a call to action to make changes in your perceptions and reactions to life.

HINT: Most people do not want to be around a "Control Freak:"

Do you know anyone in your family or social circle who must make all of the decisions about where to go for dinner, or what movie to see, or even what car you should buy? The infamous Control Freak! This person is usually bored with his/her life or really feels that people need to have her/him in control. There is also a theory in the psychology field that this person may personally feel out of control (consciously or unconsciously), and by controlling others and their environment so closely, they feel more in control.

YOUR BODY

Well if you have hit 65, you probably already have noticed changes in your body. It is almost inevitable that we will sag, wrinkle, creak and have skin issues.

HINT: **Hairs** may appear where and when you least expect them:

This is more of a male issue, but not totally. Out of nowhere 2-inch hairs stick out of your ears or eyebrows. Those hairs were not there yesterday, were they? It is a mystery. So, pluck them out with tweezers, or cut them with little scissors, or get one of those little battery run hair trimmers that stick up into your nose or into your ears. But whatever you do, please trim them. It is difficult to hold a conversation with someone when you are faced with a 2- or 3-inch hair protruding from someone's nostril or eyebrow or nose.

HINT: Give permission to your spouse or someone close to give you the hair report:

It would be great if you had someone who could safely and nicely point out to you that you have an alien hair growing on your chin, or wherever. Try to find that person, and do not be offended when they point it out.

HINT: Go to the Barber at least once a month if not more often:

Women are usually much better about grooming than men, especially when it comes to the hair on their head. Men do you realize how bad the back of your neck looks with all that curly grey hair on it? It is not sexy or appealing in any way. If you cannot get your spouse to give the back of your neck a quick shave once a week, it is going to start looking nasty soon.

HINT: Men really need to shave Daily:

Even if you are retired, unless you are a mountain man, or on an extended camping trip with your buddies, please shave daily. It is not attractive to see that stubble, and it will give you something to do each day. (It even makes your face more kissable.)

HINT: Brown spots, growths, and skin tags appear magically:

If you escape spots and growths and skin tags, then I hope you are grateful. Your Dermatologist will usually remove **skin tags**, or you can go to YOUTUBE and see different ways to do it at home. But if you get **brown spots and crusty growths,** common for people of some cultures, you will have to live with them or see a plastic surgeon. Some beauty products are available to bleach out some brown spots, but you could spend a king's fortune on creams and potions to remove wrinkles and spots and not see much change. There are some products that have helped people with brown spots, but I would suggest seeing a cosmetologist for a consultation.

A good dermatologist is worth his/her weight in gold. Not only can they keep your skin cancer free, but they can offer advice about skin issues you may have, and the dermatologist may lead you to some helpful solutions. As we age, most of us could benefit by going to a dermatologist at least once a year, but I suggest twice.

HINT: We all wrinkle:

It is difficult looking into the mirror and seeing your mom's or grandmother's face looking back at you. Your wrinkles do not have to define you. You could spend a great deal of money going through plastic surgery to have a youthful-looking face, but sadly most of us can see that you "had some work done." If it makes you feel better about yourself, and you can afford it, do it. If not, live with your wrinkles with class. You earned them, but do not wear them as a badge of honor. Let people see your heart and your loving personality clearer than your wrinkles.

HINT: Get prepared for some sagging:

Most people cannot escape the sagging underarms, the sagging breasts, and rear-end that happens as we age. You can stay fit, and it may help you some, but a little pouch above the belt or below the belt also develops for most people. Weight changes may have some effect on sagging and pouches, but this is quite a common phenomenon for people as they age no matter what their weight.

HINT: Get dressed everyday:

There will always be days when we do not want to get out of bed, or even get dressed. It may be that you do not feel well, or you are tired, or depressed. Get up, bathe, shave, and get dressed. Face the day head on. Do not bury your head in the pillow. You will feel better in clean clothes, whether you are going somewhere or not. If you must have a reason to get dressed, then go to the store for milk.

TECHNOLOGY

This is certainly a different world than what we grew up in as teens. Today the world is run by technology, and if you are not savvy, you are left behind. We really need to learn how to operate new televisions, cell phones, computers, tablets, and laptops. We also are faced with amazing new technology in cars today.

Televisions

Many seniors have trouble learning how to use the remotes for their new televisions. No, it is not as simple as before. You will have to sit and read the directions or go onto YouTube to read about your remote's operation. In my home, we have 3 remotes to operate our television. (That is just too much.) One turns the TV on and off. Another controls the sound system. Another is an Amazon Firestick that connects me to the streaming services to which we subscribe. There was quite a learning curve to be proficient at using these devices.

If you are in the market for a new television, find one that is size appropriate for your room. You do not need a mammoth television set. If you want your set mounted on the wall, you may have to pay extra for the mounting brackets and to have someone come to do the actual mounting. As I have said earlier, the new flat screen televisions do not always have the best sound, as the speakers are much smaller.

HINT: You may choose to invest in a Sound Bar that plugs into the back of your television:

A sound bar enhances the music, the background noise, and the voices.

You already know that you will need to have cable, dish, streaming or antenna access to watch your television. It has gotten expensive for many people to watch television, so they are looking for alternatives to cable.

New televisions, Smart TVs, are all made to log on to the internet automatically, so you just must sign in on the television one time when you first set it up. If you are getting internet, you can get YouTube videos for free. There are also Streaming services like Hulu (https://www.hulu.com/welcome?orig_referrer=https%3A%2F%2Fsearch .yahoo.com%2F) and ATTNow, (https://www.atttvnow.com/) which let you stream channels over the internet to your television. The prices for these and other services cost a little less than cable but may not always be as dependable.

You may also ditch cable and other services and get an Indoor Digital HGTV antenna that attaches to the back of your television and mounts up on a place high up on the wall. It is like today's "rabbit ears." Most people get up to 25-45 channels for free. Amazon Prime (https://answers.yahoo.com/question/index;_ylt=AwrC1DGi5cVdA3YA0A 9PmolQ;_ylu=X3oDMTByOHZyb21tBGNvbG8DYmYxBHBvcwMxBHZ0aWQ DBHNlYwNzcg--?qid=20120410032146AAy2djX) offers movies for free to members (and also some for a fee) that you can stream to an internet-able television, that is, a Smart TV.

Computers

A computer today is almost, but not quite, a necessity. If you have access to internet service, your computer can serve as your television, your encyclopedia, your live video connection to friends and family all over the world, your source for news, and for entertainment. You can even order groceries to be delivered by using your computer. As I sit here writing this paragraph on my laptop, I cannot remember what it was like without a computer.

A computer is a personal thing. Some seniors are still afraid of computers, while others I speak with are adept at using their iPad and have little other computer contact. Yes, an iPad is considered a computer. In fact, you can have a "tower" or desktop computer, a laptop computer, a tablet, and a cell phone all performing basically the same tasks. I use my iPad for Kindle books that I read, and this new laptop I am using folds up into a tablet.

HINT: Look for Computer Classes in local schools:

If you need help, ask for it. It will not come knocking at your door. Some stores even offer tutoring or classes for their products. Apple stores offer classes on all Apple products. Some community centers offer classes. Are you near a community college or university? Check if they offer classes for seniors or classes to audit so you can sharpen your computer skills.

Hint: Trade a friend for his/her computer tutoring:

Cook dinner or find a service you can do for your computer savvy friend in exchange for his helping you learn how to use your computer. Most people do genuinely want to help others, but we need to ask for help or we will not get it. That is one of the biggest problems I see with seniors - they will not ask for help. Instead, they suffer or go without. Please reach out and get help when you need it, even if it is only for computer training.

A friend offered me her personal story on computers: "As we grow older, we realize that we have gathered a lot of 'personal history' and at some point, someone might want to learn about it. I have frequently wished I could ask my mother or father a genealogy question, but alas, they have died and their knowledge has gone with them. I have found my computer to be invaluable in joining genealogy sites where I can glean new information, photos, and history, as well as share some of my own information with others. I have even met family members I did not know were out there, and the socialization has been rewarding.

I am creating a book of my childhood memories for my grandchildren. I have included photographs and stories. Again, my computer has been an invaluable tool. Having been born in 1943 and growing up in the '40s, '50s, etc., I have witnessed many cultural, social, and product evolutions, including the computer, the Internet, and cell phones! Take advantage of these conveniences! Having projects like these stimulate one's brain and may even add to one's social life. No matter the age of one's grandchildren, they will eventually appreciate your efforts."

Cell Phones

Almost everyone I know has canceled his/her land-line phone. It has become too expensive and redundant. All we really need is a cell phone. A cell phone is a computer in a tiny package. With a cell phone you can stream movies, set alarms, keep your schedule of appointments, text, take pictures and movies, read a book, listen to a book, listen to music, look up how old that singer or actor is, get explicit directions to anywhere, learn a new language, find out the weather here and everywhere, and even make phone calls. (On some phones you can even look at the person with whom you are chatting—"Facetime" on Apple phones.)

Cell phones are amazing technology and they are really nothing to be frightened by.

HINT: When you buy a cell phone, insist they show you how to use it:

Go back to the store if you have questions later. If you buy an iPhone, go to the Apple store, and get all the help you need. You can always ask a teenage relative or neighbor for help, but they do not always have the patience that we need as seniors. When I think I have seriously damaged my cell phone, I go to YouTube and type in a question about what is wrong with the phone and up pop several videos that address my particular phone and that issue. I usually fix my own problem.

HINT: Clean your cell phone occasionally:

Cell phones gather bacteria when you place them on tables at restaurants, or anywhere you set them down. If someone else uses your cell phone, they leave their bacteria on your phone too. Get some wipes that you can use with which to sterilize your phone on a regular basis.

HINT: Cell phone Apps are great to have:

Cell phones have **apps** available to them. Apps is short for applications. These are handy shortcuts to, for example, find directions (google maps), or apps for keeping your schedule, or interpreting another language or thousands of other practical and fun things. Most apps are free. Ask your friends what apps they use. At the end of the book I will recommend a few apps with which you might not be familiar, but you might find helpful.

Most cell phone service companies where you purchase your phone will give you some limited education as to the use of your cell phone, but it will be up to you to learn more. I happen to prefer Apple phones, only because I can also get free help at the local Apple store to fix something or learn something more about my phone.

HINT: Do not use your Cell Phone in any way while Driving:

Do not text and walk on the sidewalk. Do not walk around while you are face to face (Facetime) talking with someone on the phone. Do not answer the phone while having lunch with friends, or at the movie, or at the doctor's office. Do turn your ringer off when you are in the company of others. (If it is important, people will leave you a message if you do not answer—just like the good old days)

HINT: You do not need to Speak Loudly into a Cell Phone:

It is somewhat awkward and often annoying being around someone who is speaking loudly into a cell phone. Cell phones are amazing pieces of technology and can pick up sounds very well. So please speak normally into a cell phone when you are in public. You may find that those funny faces people were making at you when you were talking to your friend about her urinary problems will disappear if you speak at a normal level. Try it.

I could go on here about the conversations that I have overheard in restaurants, on public transportation, and even in restrooms, but I know you have all experienced those situations too. Hopefully, we will agree, there is a time and a place for talking on cell phones, no matter what your status in life.

CARS

New cars today have backup cameras and sensors all around to warn of accidents. Many cars even warn if you may be changing lanes. These are technologically advanced automobiles that are being highly recommended for seniors to drive. Many cars will stop automatically if you are driving too fast as you approach another car at a stop sign or traffic light. I have experienced sudden stops backing up and going forward in these new technologically advanced cars. It is scary! It is shocking! It also is eye-opening, as it makes you more aware as you drive.

HINT: Pay attention to the road when you drive:

As we drive, all our attention should be on driving. It should not be about the music playing, or the conversation with someone in the car, or reaching for a phone, or checking the GPS. Driving takes great concentration to not have an accident. As we age it is more common to get easily distracted as we drive. (Although this does not exclude some younger adults who are distracted drivers with phone in hand.) Some of us even have vision changes that make driving more dangerous. AARP offers a senior driving course that entitles you to an insurance discount when you successfully complete the class. I highly recommend this course.   Here is a link to the AARP course: (www.aarp.org/benefits-discounts/all/driver-safety)

HINT: There may be a day that you must give up your driver's license:

You or someone you love may have to relinquish your driver's license sometime in the future. It is not that uncommon that aging issues, physical impairments, and especially vision impairments may cause the loss of a driver's license. This is a tremendous shock to anyone-to have to give up their driver's license.

I was in the ophthalmologist's office a few years back and overheard the doctor tell a male patient that he would no longer be able to drive. (He had a friend drive him to that appointment.) He broke down and cried and moaned about his lack of freedom. It was quite sad. This happens more often than you think, but some say not enough. We must consider not only our safety, but the safety of others on the road. With today's car services like Uber and Lyft, and some community car services offered by the county or city for seniors, it is easier than ever to get around.

SOCIALIZATION

As we age, we lose people. We no longer have co-workers to socialize with all day. Friends and family move or die. We may even move to a new area that is warmer or less populated. Many things change, yet we always need companionship. We need to socialize.

I have placed this as a category of its own, as it is so important for our mental health. We need friends. We need people of our own kind, whatever that means to you. Many people go to church for socialization and that is all. If your church has many activities and groups to attend, that is great.

<u>HINT: Look up Meetup online:</u>

Here is a link to Meetup: <u>https://www.meetup.com/topics/single-seniors-socializing/</u>

There is an organization online that is called MeetUp. Look it up and see if there are activities near you. Examples of MeetUp groups might be book clubs, collector's clubs, knitting clubs, etc. It is also very simple for you to create your own Meetup group and see if you can get a few people together every other week to study birds, or exchange mango recipes, or succulent plant collecting and growing, or practicing some gentle exercise like Qigong. One of my clients started a group that meets twice a month to listen to an opera and then discuss it.

HINT: Check out what is at your local library:

Libraries offer classes and are a great way to stay connected. They also offer a great way to keep your brain stimulated.

HINT: Attend Church:

You may already go to church. Have you found one that meets your spiritual needs and your friendship needs? Today churches have study groups, book clubs, and many weekly activities where you can meet likeminded people. Some churches have large singles' groups, even for seniors. (Beware--- just because it is held in church, it does not mean that members of a singles' group all have your best interest in mind.) I know several people who attend one church to meet their spiritual needs, and another for socialization.

HINT: Find Senior or Community Centers:

If you are in a more urban area, you are likely to have community centers nearby. Do your research. Look online, ask neighbors, check the local newspaper. Community centers cater to the community, so there probably are some senior groups. You might also be able to volunteer there. I have a friend who attends quilting classes and is enrolled in knitting classes at her community center.

HINT: Get a dog to walk around the neighborhood:

If you have the time and energy for a dog and you live in a good dog walking neighborhood, then you can meet people. People who have dogs tend to love other dogs and the people who walk them. Over time, as you walk your dog in the neighborhood, you become more familiar with neighbors you did not know and might even have that neighbor over for coffee some time. If you are unable to have a dog, you might volunteer to walk the dog of a friend/neighbor while he/she is at work. Or you might consider a dog-walking service for pay.

Hint: Using Social Media to Socialize:

If you are internet savvy you can socialize on Facebook, Instagram, Twitter, or many other sites. Using social media sites is a way to stay in contact, share pictures, and send greetings to and with relatives and friends who have moved far away. However, social media sites are not necessarily intimate ways of communication. There is no emotion attached to a typed greeting, even if there is an emoji.

My recommendation is to use the internet and its access to social media sites to communicate about not so intimate things, like posting graduation pictures, or sharing pictures of grandchildren. You might also send birthday or holiday greetings to an acquaintance whom you never see anymore.

Here is a link to the Top Ten Social Media Sites for Seniors: https://www.selfgrowth.com/articles/top-10-social-networks-for-seniors

HINT: Try to use your phone more or have face to face contact for socializing.

Actual physical contact is so much more rewarding than waiting for hours or days to have someone respond to a text, or a Facebook message, etc. There is some evidence of increased depression for those who spend too much time on their computers, even on Social Media sites. Please find ways of having actual physical contact with other human beings. You will almost always feel uplifted after a lunch, or coffee with a friend or friends.

Also, please do not stand on ceremony to wait for someone to call you. Some people have active, busy lives. So, make the call, and if there is no answer, leave a pleasant message and let them call you back.

HINT: Send someone a greeting card:

Doesn't it just brighten up your day when an actual greeting card with a handwritten message arrives in the mail? Send greeting cards to friends your age and brighten their day. If you are near a Trader Joe's market, their greeting cards are only one dollar, and they have a great selection. Try a dollar store for cards too. Or make your own. They can be personalized, will be treasured by the recipient, and will give you an activity to stay engaged. You can even have a "card-making-night" with a group of friends, where you share materials and ideas.

HINT: Don't get offended if you feel like you are Invisible:

I hear seniors complain all the time that they feel invisible in certain stores, or restaurants, or anywhere where there are mostly "younger" folks. It's bad enough that the clerk at the grocery store, or at the bank, or at the movie theatre treats you like you're a doddering old fool, but do so many of these same people have to look "right through us?" Yes, it does happen. Where it does not happen is places where you are around other "seasoned" people. (So, try not to treat the 20 to 40-year old person who talks to us like we are deaf and dumb, as if they are children who lack social graces.) We do not have to stoop to that level.

I try to use humor to get noticed or attention from the young people who look through me. We go to a taco place most Tuesdays for Taco Tuesdays. It is a special price and the food is good. It is staffed totally by 20-something year old women. They used to be very businesslike with us as we placed our order and then asked for the name to be called out to bring us the food. We started using funny names, like "Rapunzel," as I am totally bald. They enjoyed our humor and became quite friendly with us as they waited to hear the name which we created each week.

HINT: You do not need to prove your intellect or fitness to anyone:

We don't need to prove our intellect and fitness to anyone, but if you like sarcasm, you may come up with a line or two when you feel like you are being treated like you are senile: "Oh, excuse me, could you tell me that again, but pretend you are talking to someone who is 40 years old?" "You must work with little children, the way you talk to people?" Of course it's hard to say that without sounding sarcastic, and sarcasm certainly isn't nice, so it might be better to talk to a manager instead, and just suggest a chat with the person on how to speak to people who she/he perceives to be one step away from the grave. These younger folks might just need a little intervention by a boss to teach them good communication skills that they are not learning from having their heads buried in social media all day.

TRAVEL

At 65 years of age and older, many of us find ourselves with more free time and maybe a budget to do a little traveling. Traveling as we age takes a little more planning than when we were 30 years old. No longer can we stuff a backpack with a few items and take off. We must make sure all of our prescriptions are filled and can last for the length of the trip. We need comfortable shoes and clothing. We need to plan everything more carefully.

HINT: A Good Travel Agent is Priceless:

If you have a travel agent to help you plan, he or she will know what you can do physically and remind you of the stresses of a proposed trip or cruise. Travel agents also know when and how to get senior discounts on cruises, trains, and planes. Travel agents offer choices of travel insurance, which I highly recommend. If you do not have a travel agent, maybe a friend who travels a great deal could share the name of an agent he or she uses.

Group tours are usually a bargain and are often all-inclusive. Tour groups like Gate One Travel offer many, many group tours all over the world. They have great tour guides and you often meet many wonderful new people in your group. Almost all tour group sites give you an idea of how strenuous the trip will be, including how much walking is involved. There are several group tour agencies listed in the Resource Section at the end of this guide.

HINT: A travel agent may get you a better deal on a cruise than the Cruise line agent can:

We see advertisements everywhere for deals on cruises. Even the big box stores like Costco, and BJ's offer great deals on cruises. If you do some comparison shopping, and I hope you do, you may find that your travel agent can access all the same offers and even beat the deals offered by these companies. I have found great deals on last minute cruise sites, but my travel agent can also find those prices, and I do not have to do the research online.

HINT: Pack a "Florence Nightingale bag":

Are you going to be away for a week or more? Make and take a special toiletry bag that is filled with cold tablets, sea sickness pills, pain pills, antacid, band aids, allergy pills, first aid ointment, ear plugs, eye drops, lip balm, alcohol wipes, and maybe even an anti-biotic prescribed by your physician. You may even have a bottle of Xanax, or muscle relaxers to throw in which might come in handy.

HINT: Get Travel Insurance for your Flights and Trips:

I do not really want you to spend money unnecessarily, but after 73 years on this planet I have heard too many stories of people having health issues happening on the road. It does not cost much more to pay for the 'gamble' that you will not need the travel insurance. By the way, most travel insurance also protects your hotel reservation and airline reservation if you have pre-paid them and suddenly you need surgery or other health emergency. I highly recommend purchasing travel insurance after hearing about so many people who have benefited from it. Here is the link to the section in the back of the book on travel insurance: *Read the information about travel insurance for seniors in the reference section.*

HINT: Buy some sterile wet wipes for travel:

When you fly, wipe down your armrests, seat table and seat belt buckle with sterile wipes. There is a great deal of bacteria in airplanes, and the seat areas certainly are not cleaned thoroughly. As we age, our immune system is often suppressed, so anything you can do to keep the bacteria from getting on your hands and face will help you stay healthy. Here's one example of isopropyl alcohol wipes that I like to travel with: (https://www.amazon.com/MG-Chemicals-Isopropyl-

AlcoholLength/dp/B008OA8LK4/ref=sr_1_17?keywords=isopropyl+alcoh
ol+wipes&qid=1573769757&s=hpc&sr=1-17)

HINT: Wash your hands frequently:

Wash your hands frequently when you travel and when you have been out shopping or playing with the grandchildren. Anything you can do to prevent cold and flu germs from being unwelcome guests on your skin is important. Most grocery stores now offer wet wipes to wipe down the handle of your grocery cart. Why? Because the person before you may have left some cold germs or bacteria on the handle that you do not wish to take with you on your hands.

YOUR HOME

If you are 65 years old or older, it is time to start making your home safer for yourself. If you are still handy and can do the work---great. If not, there are many new services available with reliable handymen and handywomen who can change some electrical things for you at a reasonable fee. A neighbor may have a handyman recommendation, or someone at church may know someone who does the work you need.

You may have noticed that your balance is not the same as it used to be. You may have noticed that if you sit on the floor, it is a little more difficult to get up than a few years back. You may have noticed that your upper body strength is less than what it was. You may have even noticed a change in your vision or hearing. If you have not noticed those changes, please be aware that they are common changes as we age.

There is no magic crystal ball to tell you when you may experience these changes, but the odds are better than winning the Lotto that you will experience some of these changes as you age. So, get prepared.

HINT: Clean out the Garage:

For safety sake, get rid of things or organize things so that you will not trip. Recovering from a broken bone after 65 is not as easy as when we were teens. Have a garage sale and get rid of stuff others may use, and things that you are done with.

Make a deal with your spouse or a friend that you will not climb a ladder to clean out the gutters without someone there with you. Make a contract with someone that you will never climb up on the roof again. It is time to start paying someone to do the work that you used to do but could potentially harm yourself doing now? Is your garage well-lit when you walk into it at night? If not, fix the lighting.

HINT: Outside Lights are Important:

Are your outside garage lights or lights by the front door bright enough? Do they come on with timers? Are they motion activated? Are they the kind that come on at dusk and stay on until daylight? These are all options. Each one is a possibility for you to use to be safer and feel safer.

Get LED lights for outside. They are more expensive, but they last a long time. If you use LED lights with a dimmer or some timers, you may have to check when you purchase them to see if these LED lights work with that feature. So, just as the inside of your house needs to have lighting to keep you safe from tripping or falling, the outside needs to be well lit enough for the same reason.

If you live in an apartment or a condo, you still need to have good lighting by your entrance door. If you need help installing new lighting or electrical fixtures, ask for help or seek out a professional.

HINT: A Video Doorbell is great:

There are several video doorbells on the market now that, once installed, will ring to your cell phone. You can then see who is at the door and talk with them from your phone. Unless you are very handy, you will probably need to have it installed, as you want it attached to your electricity and your internet. I was once traveling out of state when someone rang my doorbell in Florida. I answered and could see the UPS driver on my cell phone and asked him to leave the package at the door, as I was "indisposed." I then called someone to come pick up the package for me. This is a very handy piece of technology.

I cannot recommend these doorbells enough.

HINT: Install Grab bars:

A grab bar installed by your bathtub so you can get up easier is essential as you age. Even if you have a walk-in shower, a grab bar is good to have in there to hold onto for balance issues. They are easy to install for a professional but needs to be done correctly so that they are anchored strongly into the wall. I have even been in bathrooms when I travel where they have grab bars next to the toilet to assist in standing. That is a great idea.

HINT: Be Careful with Throw Rugs:

Throw rugs are one of the most dangerous things in your home. Besides tripping on car bumper stop in parking lots, throw rugs are extremely dangerous items to trip over or slip on. If your throw rugs are not on nonstick surfaces, consider buying new ones that will not slip, or buying the material to put under a rug that makes it non-slip. Lift your feet when you walk. Do not shuffle. Shuffling onto a throw rug could create a dangerous fall.

If you can do without throw rugs, it might be a good idea.

HINT: Be Cautious on Step stools or Step Ladders:

I'm not sure I could live without my step ladder to get up to the top shelf of the closet, or to change a light bulb. The problem as we age is that once we are up on that step stool doing whatever it is, we are doing, we sometimes forget we are 2 feet up, and we just step off into the air. BOOM! Be careful and cautious using step stools and step ladders.

PERSONAL SAFETY

Many of the items listed for the home above are about keeping you safe. There are more things to consider.

HINT: It's difficult to admit to our limitations:

It is not as if we awake one morning and find ourselves unable to lift an item that we always lifted before. It is a gradual process, yet we discover it suddenly. That limp you have had for weeks, or months really needs to be addressed. Do you need a cane for balance, or support, then get one?

Do not put off taking care of the changes that you are experiencing physically. My sister waited until she had bone rubbing on bone in her hip before she went to the specialist. Of course, he recommended hip replacement surgery and she had it done. She is athletic and active and was not happy for a few weeks of her recovery, but one year later she forgets how long she did not play tennis, as she is playing 6 days a week now. She also forgets how difficult it was doing physical therapy and walking with a cane for a few weeks. It is interesting how we can forget pain and discomfort.

Some limitations may never go away, like the loss of upper body strength. We might have been in an accident and have a limp that we are saddled with forever. We might have lost vision in one eye, or impaired hearing. Do not hide away from society or isolate from family and friends. Do not let your limitations define you. If you need a cane to walk with, get out there and walk with it. If you need hearing aids, join the hundreds of thousands of other people going out with hearing aids in their ears. If your vision changes make driving impossible, get someone else to drive, or call an Uber.

I had an elderly client years ago that lived in a "senior community" near my office. I was surprised to see her cane all decorated in fake jewels and ribbons. She said everyone loves it and does not ask her why she uses a cane, but instead they ask how they can get one like it. She took orders from strangers and made canes both for fun and a little spending money.

If you live alone and have balance issues, you might consider the purchase of one of those alarms you wear that calls someone to tell them that you have fallen. There are so many on the market, but here is an example of one: Medical alert button: (https://www.amazon.com/Senior-HELP-Dialer-Medical-Alert/dp/B00MX4NVF2/ref=pd_sbs_121_6/143-2955689-7330731?_encoding=UTF8&pd_rd_i=B00MX4NVF2&pd_rd_r=03a1e016-f7d1-44ed-a856-c567859f5e0c&pd_rd_w=ZrA8B&pd_rd_wg=8k7QI&pf_rd_p=52b7592c-2dc9-4ac6-84d4-4bda6360045e&pf_rd_r=0JAC7JHMDMDN95ES53FA&psc=1&refRID=0JAC7JHMDMDN95ES53FA

HINT: You may need to take action to avoid being victimized:

The elderly are often the victims of scams on the phone or in a parking lot. Do what you tell the little children to do: "Don't talk to strangers!" Your compassion can get you caught up in someone else's game. Give money only to those you know. Sadly, there are some people in this world that do take advantage of other people's weaknesses, or vulnerabilities.

Some elderly folks are now carrying alarms on their key rings that make extremely loud noises. If someone grabs a purse or tries to steal from you, you hit the alarm and alert everyone nearby. That will dissuade many a purse-snatcher. You can look at them here: Purse alarm: (https://www.amazon.com/s?k=purse+alarm+siren&crid=3AMYL9G36NVPX&sprefix=purse+alarm%2Caps%2C185&ref=nb_sb_ss_i_4_11)

Dr. Richard L. Travis

LEGAL AND FINANCIAL

I am not an attorney or a financial planner, so the hints that I have in this section are just practical hints that I have discovered in talking with other seniors. If you are married or in a relationship, you must protect your spouse/partner in every way in case something should happen to you. Unfortunately, so many things need to be done, that some of these things are forgotten or put aside until a later time. (Hopefully not too late.)

HINT: Pre-Plan your Funeral Arrangements:

If it is at all possible, make your funeral arrangements and put it all together into the large envelope for your spouse/heirs. A friend recently told me that when her elderly mother died a few years ago the best thing that her mother had done for her was to have all her funeral arrangements made and clearly spelled out for her. She told me that she was so grief-stricken that this arrangement made dealing with her mother's death a great deal easier.

HINT: Start Researching Social Security Benefits when you are 61 years old.

There are so many options for taking your Social Security Benefits, so you really need to be prepared. You can take reduced benefits when you are 62 years old. You may be eligible for Social Security benefits on your spouse's contributions. You may be able to wait until 67 years old to get the full benefit or even 70 years old to get the peak amount per month from your Social Security benefits. You must do the research. The time sneaks up on you fast, so read about it, or talk to an expert, but do it when you are 61 years old so you can make an informed decision.

There are widow's benefits, survivor's benefits, even children's benefits. So, please get informed. *There are some informative links at the end of this book.*

HINT: Protect all your Bank Accounts:

Even those us who are not wealthy have checking accounts and savings accounts with balances. These accounts probably should be joint accounts if you are married or have a partner. If not, another option might be to have a beneficiary listed at the bank for each account in case of your death. If a savings account of 3 or 4 thousand dollars is in your name only, and you die, most states will make that go into probate. That will take time and money to release that balance to your spouse or heirs.

You might also consider having a trust and making the trust the beneficiary of all your bank accounts. You would need an attorney to help you draw up the trust, so first find out if your financial situation warrants the expense of setting up a trust.

If your accounts are accessible by computer, make sure that your spouse or someone close to you has access to your book of passwords. A password book is a must if you have different accounts to access. I pay all my bills online, so I have a plethora of passwords for utility companies and credit card companies, in addition to bank accounts.

HINT: Keep all Your Financial Paperwork in a Folder Easily Found:

You could find a large manila folder which can hold your most important documents and keep it in a place that will be easily found. Keep a copy of your will in it. Keep a copy of the statement from each bank account you have in it. Keep any insurance policy information in it that is life or accident insurance related. You may even keep passwords or codes in it.

This envelope could save a great many headaches for your spouse or survivors if something should happen to you. This is also where you might have a handwritten sheet of paper who gets what jewelry or furniture, or even the car, if it is not totally spelled out in your will.

HINT: Have a Will and a Living Will made:

A will is relatively inexpensive to have done at an attorney's office. You can even download forms online to do your own will and have it notarized. You might consider having a Living Will made, to help your spouse or survivors if you are hospitalized in serious condition. Your family physician needs to have a copy of this. You can also download a copy of a Living Will online, or have it done at an attorney's office along with your will. A will and Living Will should probably cost from $300 to $500 at an attorney's office.

There are offices in my area, where Paralegals write up wills and Living Wills at a much-reduced fee. Check and see if there are any where you live. *I have included several sites where you can learn about whether you should have a Trust or a Will and even how to download a Will for you to complete.*

HINT: Look carefully at all your Credit Cards:

I was having dinner recently and struck up a conversation with a lovely lady at the next table. During our conversation, she said her husband had died 3 years before and she found out she had no credit rating. She was a signer on the credit cards, but not a joint owner of the account. When he died, she lost all access to her credit cards and had to apply for credit for the first time.

Make sure both you and your spouse, or someone you love, is joint owner of the credit card account. If this is confusing, just call your credit card company with the phone # on the back of the card and ask them what would happen if.... They will direct you to do the right thing to protect both you and your spouse.

Make sure both spouses are credit worthy. By the way, if you are both signers on different accounts and one of you tragically dies, the other is responsible for the debts.

HINT: Find out How your Home is Deeded:

Find out from your mortgage company or your attorney how your home is deeded. It should be put into your will. If it is not in your will, it will also go into probate and take months and some money to get it resolved to go to your heirs. There are other ways to protect your spouse with your deed, like Right to Survivorship.

I believe the best investment a senior can make is getting legal advice about a will and any property you own. In many areas of the country, the county government offers free legal services for seniors, the handicapped, or people with low income. See if that service is available for you.

This applies to a lease for an apartment too. Make sure that as we get older, both names are on the lease. We do not want to be kicked out of our apartments if our spouse dies, and we find that our name is not on the lease.

HINT: Keep Pension plan and Social Security Information in that Large Envelope:

The large envelope should also hold a copy of all your important financial documents in case someone needs to access it. If you have an IRA, please keep one statement about it in this folder. By the way, if you do have an IRA, I hope you have a beneficiary set up. Survivor benefits for your Social Security and Pension information are especially important to your surviving spouse.

What should you store in that special large envelope?

1. A copy of your Will, or Trust, and your Living Will.

2. Copies of all insurance plans related to Accidental Insurance or Life Insurance. You might even have a small plan through your credit union or credit card. I know I do.

3. Deed to the house or condo, and perhaps the Title to the car.

4. A copy of a monthly statement that has the entire account number on it of every bank or credit union account, and every credit card account.

5. Loan documents of any outstanding loans.

6. Pension, Social Security, and IRA information. Again, just a cover sheet with account numbers, and maybe phone numbers on each sheet.

7. If you have an attorney, and or a financial advisor, keep their business cards in this envelope.

8. Any special funeral arrangement and wishes.

9. Any special gifts to be made to people, like your jewelry, etc.

If you have the envelope filled with all the above information, sit with your spouse, and go over it. Also, check it every 2 or 3 years to see if things have changed. You may have paid off a loan or the house since you put this paperwork together. Another thought would be to have a safety deposit box to store all this paperwork, in case of fire or storm damage of your home.

Your passcode book and checkbooks should be stored in a safe place, but not necessarily in this envelope. You should not need to go rummaging through the large envelope often.

Every time I travel, I leave a small envelope addressed to my sister on my desk in front of my computer screens. I tell her in a note where things are in case something untimely happens to me. She would then find the large envelope and deal with the Will and the other items inside. I used to think that doing this was morbid, until I started hearing horror stories of people tragically being killed or dying at comparatively young ages and in good health.

DEATH AND DYING

The fact that we all will die someday is not to be denied. Science has not yet developed the technology that will keep us in some frozen state until the cures for old age or cancer can be found.

HINT: It can be painful and lonely getting older:

If you have children and one of them dies before you, there is great, great pain. There is no preparation for this pain. If you are in a relationship or married, and your spouse or partner dies before you do, there is great, great pain. No one prepares you for this.

As we age, we lose animals, friends, parents, family members, neighbors, our favorite actor or author or politician. It is an era of losing dear things when we get past 65 years of age. Some losses we expect, some not so much. No one has ever told me they were prepared for the loss. A spouse or friend might have a long illness, and you can be supportive and present, but if that person might die, there is still a great sense of loss.

HINT: Anti-depressants can help with grief:

There is no magic formula for getting rid of or working through grief. It takes as long as it takes to grieve. The absolute best thing to do is actively grieve. That means talk about the loss. (Cry and scream if you can.) Attend a grief group. Most Hospices have them; even many local hospitals and community centers have grief groups.

If you are inconsolable, speak to your physician about getting therapy and an anti-depressant.

HINT: Allow yourself to cry:

You don't have to be ashamed of crying. Do not be surprised if a television program, or commercial or movie evokes some sudden emotion from you. You will never be totally free from the loss, so allow an occasional sad time to pass.

HINT: Get a journal:

Write in it about how you feel each day. Or write a letter twice a week to the person who has died. When you feel like you are feeling stronger, burn the journal or letters in a little ceremony, not allowing others to ever read your sad musings.

If you have a yard, plant a tree or flowering bush in memory of the person who has died.

Get back onto your spiritual path. Attend church more often, or a prayer group, or a meditation class.

Have a ceremony with others to celebrate the life of the person who has passed.

Learn what to say to others who are grieving. What would you want to hear, and not hear? There are so many hurtful things people say, when people really do not consciously want to hurt you. They just have not learned what to say. Make what you say simple, and heartfelt, and caring. Offer to make yourself available to the grieving friend or relative.

Most people are uncomfortable around those who are grieving. Do not allow others to tell you what to do to get "better," or push you through your grief too soon. If you want to leave the photos on the wall, leave them on the wall. If you want to keep the clothes in the closet, keep the clothes in the closet. There is a time for everything. Healing is a process, and you must go through the whole process. (and everybody is different)

CONCLUSION

As you can see there is a great deal of work and effort to organize and get ready for your senior years. After you have set aside a week or even a month to get all of the paperwork together and plan what projects you want to attack in your home, you will feel relieved about all that you have accomplished.

Although it may seem morbid to start preparing for our ultimate demise, when your plans are completed, it frees you to enjoy life each day better than before. Do not forget to sit down with your spouse or partner or adult child and share all of the information in the envelope. Please share these HINTS with some of your older friends to see if you can get them on the path for a more secure retirement.

Be safe. Love life. Enjoy every moment.

Resources and References

MEDICARE INFORMATION

Medicare vs Medicaid: What is the Difference?
https://www.investopedia.com/articles/personal-finance/081114/medicaid-vs-medicare.asp

The official US Site for Medicare https://www.medicare.gov/

Social Security, Medicare Benefits:
https://www.ssa.gov/benefits/medicare/

YOUTUBE: Medicare Advantage Plans Explained:
https://video.search.yahoo.com/search/video?fr=mcafee&p=medicare.gov#id=2&vid=71a063b27572c33db372aa843ec7eaa7&action=click

YOUTUBE: Introducing the New Medicare Plan
https://video.search.yahoo.com/search/video?fr=mcafee&p=medicare.gov#id=1&vid=271fa9f90e22c44e3b3b8948200e7e5b&action=click

YOUTUBE: What is the Difference between Medicare and Medicare Advantage Plans?
https://video.search.yahoo.com/search/video?fr=mcafee&p=medicare.gov#id=5&vid=076beb685998ed1d319d4264fd2a09a5&action=view

YOUTUBE: Comparing Medicare Supplement Plans:
https://video.search.yahoo.com/search/video?fr=mcafee&p=medicare.gov#id=19&vid=234cc1538582ac209a8e1ca79ba89fc4&action=view

YOUTUBE: Medicare Benefits for Hearing Aids:
https://video.search.yahoo.com/search/video?fr=mcafee&p=medicare.gov#id=28&vid=defa5f0668f915a7223725d09425f94b&action=view

YOUTUBE: Best Medicare Supplement Plans for 2019:
https://video.search.yahoo.com/search/video?fr=mcafee&p=medicare.gov#id=48&vid=da67f9653d0b683e94784c7457b4bf5a&action=view

Get Help with Your Taxes | USAGov

www.usa.gov/help-with-taxes

GENERAL HELP FOR SENIORS

Senior | Definition of Senior by Merriam-Webster

www.merriam-webster.com/dictionary/senior

Senior Helpers

www.seniorhelpers.com

Senior assistance programs | Help for senior citizens

www.needhelppayingbills.com/html/senior.

Senior Helpers - Seniors Resource Guide

seniorsresourceguide.com/directories/National/.

Average Senior Helpers Salary | Payscale

www.payscale.com/research/US/Employer=Senior_Helpers

Senior Help Desk | Blogs, Events, Directory Listings

www.seniorhelpdesk.com

Grants to Help Senior Citizens Fix Up Their Homes | Home ...

homeguides.sfgate.com/grants-senior-citizens-fix.

Find Help – Senior Assistance – Help for the Elderly – AARP ...

www.aarp.org/aarp-foundation/find-help

Senior Helpers Telemedicine Pilot Helps Cut Costs, Reduce ER ...

homehealthcarenews.com/2019/08/senior-helpers...

SeniorPeopleMeet

www.seniorpeoplemeet.com

4 Ways to Help Senior Citizens - wikiHow

www.wikihow.com/Help-Senior-Citizens

Senior Citizen Benefits - Help for Seniors with ... - ncoa.org

www.ncoa.org/economic-security/benefits

Senior Helpers National - Posts | Facebook

www.facebook.com/seniorhelpersnatl/posts

Senior.com - Age Well, Shop Smart - The Store for Older Adults

senior.com

Get Help with Your Taxes | USAGov

www.usa.gov/help-with-taxes

Senior Home Care Equipment Products and Assistive Devices ...

www.agingcare.com/Products

Health Information - nia.nih.gov

www.nia.nih.gov/health

Senior Homeshares

www.seniorhomeshares.com

#1 Medical Alert Service in the U.S | Philips Lifeline

www.lifeline.philips.com

AARP® Official Site - Join & Explore the Benefits

www.aarp.org

Help for All Your Senior Care Needs

www.eldercaredirectory.org

Senior Housing Help | Retirement Blog from After55.com

www.after55.com/blog/category/senior-housing-help

Senior Housing Options - HelpGuide.org

www.helpguide.org/.../senior-housing.htm

Senior Assistance Programs & Services

www.centerforpositiveaging.org/senior assistance.

Payment Options & Financial Assistance for Senior Care

www.payingforseniorcare.com

HUD.gov / U.S. Department of Housing and Urban Development (HUD)

www.hud.gov/topics/information_for_senior_citizens

Florida Senior Legal Services - Florida Department of Elder ...

elderaffairs.state.fl.us/does/legal_services.php

Financial Help for Senior Citizen Debt, Housing & Employment

www.incharge.org/.../financial-help-senior-citizens
SeniorNet

seniornet.org

Retired Seniors - Volunteer | Medicare Insurance | Social ...

www.seniorcorps.org

What is a Senior Center? Facts & Benefits Most Don't Know - NCOA

www.ncoa.org/national-institute-of-senior..

Stuff Seniors Need | Free information for seniors and busy ...

stuffseniorsneed.com

CELL PHONES AND COMPUTERS

Best Cell Phone Plans for Seniors 2019:
https://www.nerdwallet.com/blog/utilities/cellphone-plan-senior-citizens/

Senior Cell Phone Plan Comparison:
https://www.moneysavingpro.com/cell-phone-plans/senior-plans/

Computer Training for Seniors:
https://www.seniorcitizensguide.com/articles/activities/senior-computers.htm

Senior Computer Classes online to try for Free:
https://www.medicare.org/articles/senior-computer-classes-to-try-online-for-free/

Top 6 Easiest Smartphones for Seniors in 2019 - Mobility With …

www.mobilitywithlove.com/easiest-smartphones-for..

The 7 Best Cell Phones for Seniors in 2019 - lifewire.com

www.lifewire.com/best-cell-phones-for-senior.

HEARING AID INFORMATION

The Best Hearing Aids of 2019: https://www.toptenreviews.com/best-hearing-aids

Hearing Aid Ratings-Consumer Reports:
https://www.consumerreports.org/cro/hearing-aids.htm

Best Hearing Aids for 2019: https://www.retirementliving.com/best-hearing-aid-companies

VISION FOR SENIORS

How vision changes as you age - allaboutvision.com

www.allaboutvision.com/over60/vision-changes.htm

Vision Problems in Aging Adults - webmd.com

www.webmd.com/eye-health/vision-problems-aging.

Your Vision in the Senior Years - webmd.com

www.webmd.com/eye-health/senior-years

Adult Vision: Over 60 Years of Age

www.aoa.org/.../adult-vision-over-60-years-of-age

Dental and Vision Insurance for Seniors

www.surebridgeinsurance.com/seniors/senior..

9 Entertaining Activities for Low Vision Seniors with ...

dailycaring.com/9-activities-for-low-vision..

The Best Vision Insurance For Seniors On Medicare

myfamilylifeinsurance.com/2017/12/27/the-best..

Senior Dental, Hearing, and Vision Plans | Senior Plans ...

www.medicaremall.com/products/senior-dental..

AARP dental and vision insurance for seniors – Dental

youngmumstufff.com/aarp-dental-and-vision.

Get free health, dental, and vision care

www.needhelppayingbills.com/html/get_free_health.

Vision – AAA Senior Driving

seniordriving.aaa.com/.../vision

Caring for Seniors with Vision Loss - Caregiver Guide to ...

www.care.com/senior-care-caring-for-seniors-with.

Hearing and Vision Loss - VisionAware

www.visionaware.org/info/for-seniors/health-and..

How to Get Dental Care and Vision Care | Medicare Made Clear

blog.medicaremadeclear.com/how-to-get-dental-and..

Telephones for the Blind/Low Vision - Assistech

assistech.com/store/telephones-for-the-blind-and..

Seniors | National Federation of the Blind

www.nfb.org/our-community/seniors

Free Glasses and Eye Exams for Seniors - Stuff Seniors Need

stuffseniorsneed.com/free-glasses-and-eye-exams-seniors

How to Make Life Easier and Safer for Seniors with Low Vision

www.agingcare.com/Articles/making-life-easier..

Hobbies for Blind and Low-Vision Seniors - AgingCare.com

www.agingcare.com/articles/hobbies-for-blind-and..

Coping With Vision Loss-Opportunities for Seniors

www.clevelandsightcenter.org/programs-services/seniors

Warning Signs of Age-Related Vision Problems

www.aplaceformom.com/blog/3-10-14-common-eye.

Top Low Vision Aids for Seniors with Vision Problems | IrisVision

irisvision.com/low-vision-aids-for-seniors-with.

Statistics about Seniors with Vision Loss | American ...

www.afb.org/.../statistics-seniors-vision-loss

Eye Care for Seniors

www.naturaleyecare.com/.../eye-care-for-seniors.asp

Night Vision and Driving: How Safe Are Older Drivers?

www.allaboutvision.com/over40/night-driving.htm

Seniors and Cataracts - Understanding This Common Vision ...

www.senioradvice.com/articles/seniors-and.

Vision, Cognition, and Mobility Challenges for Elderly Drivers

www.uspharmacist.com/article/vision-cognition.

Low Vision Aids - ActiveForever

www.activeforever.com/.../low-vision-aids

Double vision (Diplopia): Causes, diagnosis, and treatment

www.medicalnewstoday.com/articles/170634.php

Grants and Programs for Low Vision and Macular Degeneration

www.enhancedvision.com/grants-and-assistive.

Common Causes of Vision Loss in Elderly Patients - American ...

www.aafp.org/afp/1999/0701/p99.html

TEETH and EATING

Senior Oral Health - Home | ADHA

www.adha.org/.../7255_Senior_Oral_Health.pdf

Senior Dental Care - A Complete Consumer Guide

www.yourdentistryguide.com/seniors

Dental Problems in the Elderly | SeniorHealth365.com

www.seniorhealth365.com/health/dental-problems.

Teeth and Aging: How Your Mouth Changes as You Get Older

www.webmd.com/oral-health/teeth-gums-age

The aging mouth - and how to keep it younger - Harvard Health

www.health.harvard.edu/diseases-and-conditions/

Tooth Loss in Seniors | National Institute of Dental and ...

www.nidcr.nih.gov/.../tooth-loss/seniors

Aging and Your Teeth - Miami Perio

www.miamiperio.com/blog/aging-teeth

5 Top Dental Problems in Older Adults: Symptoms & Treatments ...

dailycaring.com/5-top-dental-problems-in-older.

The 15 Most Common Health Concerns for Seniors

www.everydayhealth.com/news/most-common-health.

Do Senior's Teeth Break More Easily? - AgingCare.com

www.agingcare.com/Questions/do-seniors-teeth.

Study Links Tooth Loss to Declining Health in Elderly ...

www.colgate.com/en-us/oral-health/life-stages/..

Do seniors have more problems with tooth removal and ...

www.sharecare.com/health/tooth-extraction/.

Why are Older Adults at an Increased Risk for Mouth & Gum ...

www.toothwisdom.org/a-z/article/why-are-older.

Aging and Dental Health - Make Sure Elderly Loved One Gets ...

www.deardoctor.com/articles/aging-and-dental-health

Oral hygiene for the elderly

www.elder.org/.../oral-hygiene-for-the-elderly

The Ultimate Oral Health Guide for Seniors | Toothbrush.org

www.toothbrush.org/ultimate-guide-oral-health.

Senior Health: Tips for Successful Aging - medicinenet.com

www.medicinenet.com/senior_health/article.ht

Free Dentures and Dental Care for Low-Income Individuals

stuffseniorsneed.com/free-dentures-and-free-dental-care

How to Get a Free Dental Implant - Our Senior Resources

ourseniorresources.com/free-dental-implant

Dentures vs. Implants - seniorcitizensguide.com

www.seniorcitizensguide.com/articles/chicago/.

Teeth Stains: Causes, Types, and How to Remove Teeth Stains

crest.com/en-us/oral-health/conditions/teeth.

How to Fix Aging Teeth and Receding Gums | The Fine Line

thefinelinemag.com/aging-teeth-and-receding-gums

Boston Market App: https://apps.apple.com/us/app/boston-market/id373559901

Top 5 Best Free Restaurant Apps for iPhone & Android | Heavy.com

heavy.com/tech/2015/08/top-5-best-free...

California Pizza Kitchen: https://www.cpk.com/

Panera: https://www.panerabread.com/en-us/home.html/

Denny's Rewards: https://www.dennys.com/rewards/

Best Fast Casual Restaurants: https://www.ranker.com/list/best-fast-casual-restaurants/chef-jen

Zaxbys: https://www.ranker.com/review/zaxby_s/2438113?ref=node_name&pos=23&a=0&ltype=n&l=587282&g=0

Sweet Tomatoes: https://sweettomatoes.com/

Bob Evans: https://www.bobevans.com/

Cracker Barrel: https://www.crackerbarrel.com/

GRAB BARS

Best Bathroom Grab Bars: https://bestreviews.com/best-bathroom-grab-bars

Grab Bars at Lowes: https://www.lowes.com/pl/Grab-bars-Bathroom-safety-Bathroom/4294737160

Grab Bars at Walmart: https://www.walmart.com/browse/health/grab-bars/976760_1005860_1230858_4152217_8878870

Grab Bars from Amazon: https://www.amazon.com/Bath-Shower-Grab-Bars/b?node=344743011

Shower Grab Bars at Home Depot: https://www.homedepot.com/b/Bath-Bath-Accessories-Bath-Safety-Grab-Bars/N-5yc1vZcfvb

YOUTUBE: Installing a Grab Bar in the Shower:
https://www.youtube.com/watch?v=vgaVOXIWrHE

YOUTUBE: Installing Grab Bar into Ceramic Tile:
https://www.youtube.com/watch?v=ufTSoXbW1Pw

YOUTUBE: Installing a Grab Bar:
https://www.youtube.com/watch?v=MaHDYuPX7gY

SOUND BARS

Best Sound Bars for Voice Clarity:
https://bestsoundbarfortheprice.com/best-soundbar-for-voice-clarity/

Best Soundbar for Dialogue Clarity: https://www.watchvibe.com/best-soundbar-for-dialogue-clarity/

Zvox: The Best soundbar for voice clarity:
https://zvox.com/collections/best-soundbar-for-dialogue-voice-clarity

The Best Soundbars for 2019:
https://www.pcmag.com/roundup/310925/the-best-soundbars

YOUTUBE: Installing a Soundbar for Dummies:
https://www.youtube.com/watch?v=RTqUOPTcsY4

YOUTUBE: How to Hook up a Sound Bar with an HDMI cable:
https://www.youtube.com/watch?v=vDhytwQOZfw

WILLS AND TRUSTS

Wills vs Trusts: Which are Better?
https://www.fool.com/investing/2016/11/08/wills-vs-trusts-which-are-better.aspx

Wills and Trusts: Pros and Cons of Each:
https://www.lawpmh.com/trusts-vs-wills-pros-and-cons-of-each/

Understanding the Difference between a Will and a Trust:
https://www.elderlawanswers.com/understanding-the-differences-between-a-will-and-a-trust-7888

Wills and Trusts: Legal Zoom: https://info.legalzoom.com/wills-vs-trust-4521.html

Living Trusts vs Wills: https://www.nolo.com/legal-encyclopedia/living-trust-v-will.html

5 Ways in which a Trust is better than a Will: https://ssbllc.com/five-ways-in-which-a-trust-is-better-than-a-will/

What is a Living Will?
https://www.alllaw.com/articles/wills_and_trusts/article7.asp

Free Living Will Forms: https://eforms.com/living-will/

Do your own Living Will: https://www.doyourownwill.com/living-will/states.html

How to Write my own Will: https://info.legalzoom.com/write-own-will-4007.html

Should you write your own Will? https://www.thebalance.com/should-you-write-your-own-will-3505206

Write your own Will: https://www.uslegalforms.com/wills/write-your-own-will.htm

VIDEO DOORBELLS

The best Video Doorbells in 2019:
https://www.pcmag.com/roundup/358684/the-best-video-doorbells

The best Consumer Reports video Doorbell in 2019:
https://www.consumerreports.org/video-doorbells/best-video-doorbells-of-the-year/

Amazon Video Door Bells: https://www.amazon.com/video-doorbell/s?k=video+doorbell

The Best Smart Video Doorbell: https://www.safewise.com/resources/smart-doorbell-buyers-guide/

YOUTUBE: Installing a Video Doorbell: https://www.youtube.com/watch?v=hDGdM8rIDQU

YOUTUBE: Installing a Video Doorbell without screws: https://www.youtube.com/watch?v=6U2DZJHKs7I

SOCIALIZATION

Finding a Senior Community Center near You: https://www.seniorliving.org/life/senior-center/

Senior Center Directory: https://www.seniorcenterdirectory.com/

Socialization and its Importance to Seniors: https://www.seniorly.com/resources/articles/socialization-and-its-importance-to-seniors

Senior Citizens Socializing: https://www.meetup.com/topics/single-seniors-socializing/

Social Media and Seniors: https://www.aarp.org/home-family/personal-technology/info-05-2013/seniors-social-media-technology-facebook.html

Top Ten Social Media Sites for Seniors: https://www.selfgrowth.com/articles/top-10-social-networks-for-seniors

5 Benefits of Social Media for Seniors: http://seniorcarecorner.com/5-benefits-of-social-media-for-seniors

Benefits of Socialization for Seniors - Acts Retirement www.actsretirement.org/latest-retirement-news/.

7 Ways Socializing Benefits Seniors - The HomePlace at Midway
www.homeplaceatmidway.com/7-ways-socializing.

Socialization and Its Importance to Seniors | Seniorly
www.seniorly.com/resources/articles/.

Studies Connect Socializing & Life Quality | Holiday Retirement
www.holidaytouch.com/Retirement-101/senior..

The Importance of Socialization for Seniors - Bethesda Health ...
www.bethesdahealth.org/the-importance-of..

How Socialization Can Benefit the Elderly - negeriatrics.com
www.negeriatrics.com/blog/how-socialization-can-benefit.

How Social Connections Keep Seniors Healthy - Greater Good

greatergood.berkeley.edu/article/item/how social

Senior Socialization Leads to Better Quality of Life | AASC
www.aasc.org/news/articles/2011/038_Senior_Socialization..

Seniors Social groups | Meetup

20 Facts about Senior Isolation That Will Stun You

www.aplaceformom.com/blog/10-17-14-facts-about

3 Ways to Build a Social Life as a Senior Citizen - wikiHow

www.wikihow.com/Build-a-Social-Life-as-a-Senior..

Senior Meetup | Senior Social | Senior Activities | Senior ...
www.programsforelderly.com/social-senior-meetup-senior..

Never Too Old to Find New Friends - Senior Companionship
www.aarp.org/relationships/friends/info-04-2011/..

Research Suggests a Positive Correlation between Social ...

www.nia.nih.gov/about/living-long-well-21st..

A Hot Trend: The Internet, Social Media & The Elderly

www.huffpost.com/entry/older-people-social-media...

You Are Not Alone: 6 Steps to Reduce Senior Isolation

www.aplaceformom.com/blog/9-2-14-reduce-senior...

55+ Senior Living and Retirement Communities | After55.com
www.after55.com

5 Benefits Of Social Interaction For Seniors With Dementia

www.sunriseseniorliving.com/blog/june-2016/5.

CBD OIL FOR SENIORS

Benefits of CBD Oil for Seniors: https://cbdoilchronicle.com/benefits-of-cbd-oil-for-seniors/

Top Benefits of CBD Oil for Seniors:
https://www.marijuanabreak.com/cbd-for-senior-citizens

The 3 Best CBD Products for Seniors:
https://mycbdauthority.com/2019/03/05/best-cbd-products-seniors/

7 Life Changing Benefits of CBD for Seniors: https://medium.com/cbd-origin/7-life-changing-health-benefits-of-cbd-for-seniors-958f0818bc9d

CBD Oil Reviews: https://www.cannainsider.com/reviews/cbd-oil-reviews/

Remedy Reviews of CBD for Seniors: https://timesofcbd.com/cbd-enhances-majority-seniors-cannabidiol-case-study/

5 Best CBD Oils for Sleep: https://www.marijuanabreak.com/best-cbd-oils-sleep-review

SLEEPING

Seniors and sleep: Why seniors are often sleep deprived - WebMD

www.webmd.com/.../do-seniors-need-less-sleep

Senior Sleep Guide - A Safe Sleeping Guide for Seniors ...

www.sleepreports.com/safe-sleeping-guide-for-seniors

Sleep and Aging - A Comprehensive Guide for Seniors

www.sleepadvisor.org/sleep-aging

Seniors and Sleep: Five Things You Might Not Know

aginginstride.enewsworks.com/.../Seniors-and-Sleep-Five.

Seniors and Sleep: Do People Sleep Less as They Age?

www.elevatingseniors.com/sleep-less-age

Aging & Sleep Information - National Sleep Foundation

www.sleepfoundation.org/articles/aging-and-sleep

Seniors and Sleep: How much do they need?

www.comfortkeepers.com/info-center/category/...

5 Top Causes of Sleep Problems in Aging, & Proven Ways to ...

betterhealthwhileaging.net/top-5-causes-sleep.

Sleep Disorders in the Elderly - healthline.com

www.healthline.com/health/sleep/sleep-disorders.

Sleeping Pills for Insomnia and Anxiety in Older People ...

www.choosingwisely.org/patient-resources/treating.

6 Reasons Behind an Elderly's Sleeping Too Much | New Health ...

www.newhealthadvisor.org/Elderly-Sleeping-Too.

Seniors and Sleep – Dreampad

dreampadsleep.com/pages/seniors-and-sleep

Sleep Tips for Older Adults - HelpGuide.org

www.helpguide.org/articles/sleep/how-to-sleep...

Hard Facts About Sleep Problems in the Elderly

www.aplaceformom.com/blog/2013-03-7-sleep.

Fatigue (tiredness) in elderly: Causes and how to treat it

www.belmarrahealth.com/fatigue-tiredness-elderly

A Good Night's Sleep - nia.nih.gov

www.nia.nih.gov/health/good-nights-sleep

Normal and Abnormal Sleep in the Elderly - ncbi.nlm.nih.gov

www.ncbi.nlm.nih.gov/pmc/articles/PMC3142094

Sleep and Aging - Senior Sleep Guide | Tuck Sleep

www.tuck.com/sleep-aging

2 Ways to Solve Senior Sleep Problems for Better Rest and ...

dailycaring.com/solve-senior-sleep-problems-for.

Married Couples and Sleeping Together - verywellmind.com

www.verywellmind.com/married-couples-good-nights.

Hard Facts About Sleep Problems in the Elderly

www.aplaceformom.com/blog/2013-03-7-sleep.

Insomnia in the Elderly - What You Need to Know

www.drugs.com/cg/insomnia-in-the-elderly.html

How Much Melatonin Should Senior Citizens Take to Sleep ...

seniordirectory.com/articles/info/how-much.

The dangers of sleeping pills for seniors - The Globe and Mail

www.theglobeandmail.com/life/the-dangers-of..

2 Ways to Solve Senior Sleep Problems for Better Rest and ...

dailycaring.com/solve-senior-sleep-problems-for

Seniors Sleep Problems | Sleep Wellness Doctor

www.sleepwellnessdoctor.com/seniors-sleep-problems

Sleep Changes in Older Adults - familydoctor.org

familydoctor.org/sleep-changes

What are the most popular sleeping pills for seniors?

www.insomnialand.com/the-side-effects-and.

Senior Sleep: Sleeping Habits and Napping - Disabled World

www.disabled-world.com/health/neurology/sleep.

11 Tips to Improve Senior Sleep by Reducing Pain and ...

dailycaring.com/11-tips-to-improve-senior-sleep

Why More Seniors Are Using Cannabis to Sleep | Leafly

www.leafly.com/.../seniors-using-cannabis-sleep

8 Benefits of CBD for Senior Citizens | SeniorDirectory.com

seniordirectory.com/articles/info/benefits-of.

Medical Marijuana to Improve the Sleep of Elderly | Marijuana ...

www.marijuanadoctors.com/blog/marijuana-for...

How Much Sleep Do Seniors Need? - Senior Health Center ...

www.everydayhealth.com/senior-health/how-much.

Napping: Do's and don'ts for healthy adults - Mayo Clinic

www.mayoclinic.org/healthy-lifestyle/adult.

Best Mattress for Older (Elderly) Adults - The Sleep Advisor

www.sleepadvisor.org/best-mattress-for-elderly

Fatigue in Older Adults - nia.nih.gov

www.nia.nih.gov/health/fatigue

Nocturia or Frequent Urination at Night | National Sleep ...

www.sleepfoundation.org/articles/nocturia-or..

The Importance of Quality Sleep for Seniors

www.alert-1.com/blog/general/the-importance-of.

Aging and Sleep: How Seniors Can Get a Better Night's Rest ...

seniorsathome.jfcs.org/aging-and-sleep

The Best (and Worst) Positions for Sleeping - Greatist

greatist.com/happiness/best-sleep-position

SLEEP AIDS

The Best Sleep Aids in 2019:
https://www.consumerhealthdigest.com/sleep-disorder/best-sleep-aid-supplements.html

Natural Sleep Aids and Remedies:
https://www.webmd.com/women/natural-sleep-remedies#1

Five Natural Sleep Aids that Actually Work:
https://www.wellandgood.com/good-advice/5-natural-sleep-supplements-that-actually-work/

9 Natural Sleep Aids that are backed by Science:
https://www.healthline.com/nutrition/sleep-aids

Amazon Sleep Herbal Supplement: https://www.amazon.com/sleep-herbal-supplement/s?k=sleep+herbal+supplement

FOOD

Food Assistance Programs for the Elderly | NCOA

www.ncoa.org/economic-security/benefits/food-and.

Senior Food Assistance Programs for Seniors and the Elderly

www.senior-meals.org/Senior-Food-Assistance-Programs

Older Individuals | Nutrition.gov

www.nutrition.gov/audience/older-individuals

Elderly Nutrition | Healthy Eating for Seniors | Elderly ...

www.sageminder.com/Caregiving/ElderlyNutrition.aspx

The Nutrition Needs of Senior Citizens | Everyday Health

www.everydayhealth.com/senior-health/..

Free Food Delivery Services for Seniors & Paid Senior Meal ...

www.seniorliving.org/internet/food-delivery

Older Adults and Food Safety

www.fsis.usda.gov/wps/portal/fsis/topics/food...

Senior Nutrition - Healthy Eating Tips & Resources | NCOA

www.ncoa.org/.../food-and-nutrition/senior-nutrition

Elderly Nutrition 101: 10 Foods To Keep You Healthy | Aging.com

www.aging.com/elderly-nutrition-101-10-foods-to..

Healthy Eating for Seniors - Healthline: Medical information ...

www.healthline.com/health/healthy-eating-for-seniors

Food Stamps for Seniors Resource Page - Food Stamps Now

foodstampsnow.com/food-stamps-for-seniors

Myths About Food and Nutrition After 60 - webmd.com

www.webmd.com/.../myths-facts-food-nutrition-60

10 Free Programs For Seniors That You May Not Know About ...

patch.com/new-york/northport/bp--10-free..

Food Insecurity Among Senior Citizens Growing as Population ...

www.moveforhunger.org/food-insecurity-among...

2019 Biggest List of Senior Discounts (Restaurants, Retail ...

www.theseniorlist.com/senior-discounts

Here are some of the special nutritional needs of seniors and ...

www.newsmax.com/Health/health-news/seniors-diet.

18 Quick, Easy and Healthy Meals for Seniors - Care.com

www.care.com/c/stories/5445/quick-easy-healthy.

Best Diets for Seniors | Wellness | US News

health.usnews.com/.../01/21/best-diets-for-seniors

10 Healthy Make-Ahead Meals for Seniors and Caregivers

www.sunriseseniorliving.com/blog/august-2018/10..

Why Seniors' Tastes Change with Age - AgingCare.com

www.agingcare.com/Articles/Loss-of-Taste-in-the.

5 Ways Seniors Can Have Food Delivered to Their Door ...

www.senioradvisor.com/blog/2017/04/5-ways.

Instacart deliveries from many Grocery Stores:
https://www.instacart.com/

Walmart.com

grocery.walmart.com

Deliver Lean:

www.deliverlean.com

Fresh Meal Plan:

www.freshmealplan.com

Fresh n' Lean:

www.freshnlean.com

Freshly Prepared Meals Delivered to Your Door

www.magickitchen.com

THE MIND--MENTAL FITNESS

The Importance of Mental Fitness - healthline.com

www.healthline.com/health/depression/mental-fitness

The Importance of Mental Exercise for Seniors | Tully Law, PC

tullyelderlaw.com/importance-mental-exercise-seniors

10 Brain Exercises That Boost Memory | Everyday Health

www.everydayhealth.com/longevity/mental-fitness/.

Brain Exercises for Seniors: Increase an Aging Adult's Mental ...

blog.ioaging.org/home-care/brain-exercises-for..

Seniors and signs of mental fitness slips | MassMutual

blog.massmutual.com/post/seniors-and-mental-fitness

Free Brain Exercises for Seniors | Livestrong.com

www.livestrong.com/article/135492-free-brain..

12 Best Brain Stimulating Activities for Seniors - mindhow.com

www.mindhow.com/...brain-stimulating-activities-for-seniors

Mental Fitness for Seniors | Psychology Today

www.psychologytoday.com/.../mental-fitness-seniors

LIFE Senior Services | 10 Facts About Mental Health and Aging

www.lifeseniorservices.org/seniorline/10_Facts_About...

10 Simple (and Fun!) Ways to Improve Your Mental Fitness

www.verywellmind.com/top-ways-to-improve-your

Top 15 Brain Teasers and Games for Mental Exercise | SharpBrains

sharpbrains.com/blog/2008/11/17/top-15-brain...

Brain Exercises for Dementia: How They Help The Mind

www.webmd.com/alzheimers/guide/preventing.

How Seniors Can Improve Mental Health | Stronger Seniors ...

strongerseniors.com/blogs/news/how-seniors-can..

8 Best Brain Training Websites and Games

www.verywellmind.com/top-websites-and-games-for..

3 benefits of mental exercise for seniors | Aegis Living

www.aegisliving.com/resource-center/3-benefits..

The Importance of Elderly Exercise & Socialization Programs

healthfully.com/543831-the-importance-of-elderly..

Brain Gain: Mental Exercise Makes Elderly Minds More Fit ...

www.scientificamerican.com/article/brain-gain.

5 Benefits of Technology to Share with Seniors and Their ...

www.caregiverstress.com/geriatric-professional..

Cognitive Activities for the Elderly | LoveToKnow

seniors.lovetoknow.com/Cognitive_Activities_for..

Cognitive Health and Older Adults - nia.nih.gov

www.nia.nih.gov/health/cognitive-health-and...

Four Common Mental Illnesses in the Elderly: The Factors and ...

caringpeopleinc.com/blog/mental-illnesses-in-the..

EXERCISE

The Importance of Elderly Exercise & Socialization Programs
healthyliving.azcentral.com/importance-elderly..

Top 100 Health and Wellness Sites for Seniors:
www.rncentral.com/...health_and_wellness_sites_for_seniors

Top 10 Reasons Exercise Is Important for Senior Health

wellness.nifs.org/blog/top-10-reasons-exercise..

Senior Exercise and Aging:

www.newcastleintegratedphysiotherapy.com.au/blog/.

Exercise for Older Adults: MedlinePlus:

medlineplus.gov/exerciseforolderadults.html

What are the Best Exercises for Seniors? (with pictures)

www.wisegeek.com/what-are-the-best-exercises-for..

Exercise for Seniors - How to Live Better as You Age:

www.verywellfit.com/exercise-for-seniors-1230955

 Senior Exercise: Click for Workout Routines and Ideas:

www.medicinenet.com/senior_exercise/article.htm

7 Worst Exercises for Seniors—and What to Do Instead:

www.silversneakers.com/blog/worst-senior-exercises

YouTube Fitness

Single Best Balance Exercise for Seniors and Fall Prevention:
https://video.search.yahoo.com/search/video?fr=mcafee&p=seniors+and
+exercise#id=3&vid=23335885885d3683a29eecd4ccad1b8c&action=click

Full body Flexibility Exercises for Seniors:
https://video.search.yahoo.com/search/video?fr=mcafee&p=seniors+and
+exercise#id=15&vid=a9f3c5d0c7d1458c156dc4c3030908cd&action=vie
w

Top 10 Balance Exercises at Home, STOP FALLS
https://video.search.yahoo.com/search/video?fr=mcafee&p=seniors+and
+exercise#id=24&vid=2b24d77675f225bff0623c10c97a802e&action=vie
w

How Seniors Can Benefit from Adopting an Exercise Regimen:
www.agingcare.com/Articles/Exercise-benefits-for..

Exercises for Seniors: The Complete Guide - evelo.com
www.evelo.com/exercises-for-seniors

VIDEO: 15 Minute Senior Exercise Program for Balance and ...
dailycaring.com/video-15-minute-senior-exercise.

Everyday Moves: 6 Easy Routines for Strength and Balance ...
seniorplanet.org/everyday-moves-6-easy-routines..

Senior Fitness & Exercise Programs | NCOA www.ncoa.org/center-for-healthy-aging/basics-of.

11 Exercise Ideas for Seniors - Senior Health Center ...
www.everydayhealth.com/senior-health-photos/

YOUTUBE: 15 Minute Senior Workout - Has Low Impact
www.youtube.com/watch?v=K727ao6Kjr4

Seniors and Exercise: Starting An Exercise Program ...
www.orthoinfo.org/en/staying-healthy/seniors-and

10 Simple Fall Prevention Exercises Seniors Can ... - DailyCaring
dailycaring.com/10-simple-fall-prevention.

Exercise Tips for Seniors - onhealth.com:
www.onhealth.com/content/1/senior_fitness_exercises

10 Low-impact Exercises for Seniors | HowStuffWorks:
health.howstuffworks.com/wellness/aging/senior..

YOUTUBE: Exercises for Seniors - Stretching Exercises for Seniors
...www.youtube.com/watch?v=YGRje8p5gbc

Real Life Benefits of Exercise & Physical Activity | Go4Life
go4life.nia.nih.gov/real-life-benefits-of..

18 Chair Exercises for Seniors & How to Get Started
www.vivehealth.com/.../chair-exercises-for-seniors

5 Benefits of Exercise for Seniors and Aging Adults | The ...
thegreenfields.org/5-benefits-exercise-seniors..

9 Important Stretching Exercises for Seniors to Do Every Day ...
yurielkaim.com/stretching-exercises-seniors

Healthy Exercise and Diet Plans for Seniors
www.verywellfit.com/healthy-weight-loss-for.

18 Best Exercises for Seniors: Safe Balance, Strength and ...

www.highya.com/articles-guides/best-senior.

12 Best Leg Exercises for Seniors and The Elderly | Eldergym®

eldergym.com/leg-exercises

Find Senior Exercise Information, Routines, Videos, and Advice!
www.greatseniorliving.com/.../senior-exercise

Sciatica Stretches and Exercises for Seniors
www.spine-health.com/blog/sciatica-stretches-and.

Stretching Exercises for Seniors: Improve Mobility
www.healthline.com/.../stretching exercises

9 Important Stretching Exercises for Seniors to Do Every Day ...
yurielkaim.com/stretching-exercises-seniors

7 Best Abdominal Exercises for Seniors (Do These Anywhere)
yurielkaim.com/abdominal-exercises-for-seniors

What are the best golf exercises for seniors? | HowStuffWorks
health.howstuffworks.com/wellness/aging/senior..

Workouts & Exercises for Seniors | Senior Posture
...www.seniorliving.org/life/active-senior/exercise

Exercise Tips For Seniors With Limited Mobility And Chronic ...

www.capitalsenior.com/blog/exercise-tips-seniors..

Senior Citizen Exercise Tools | LoveToKnow

exercise.lovetoknow.com/Senior_Citizen_Exercise.

5 Simple and Fun Water Aerobics Exercises for Seniors ...
www.seniorlifestyle.com/5-best-water-aerobics..

Dance Along Workout for Seniors and Elderly - Low Impact ...
www.pinterest.com/pin/50313720807753064

APPS FOR SMART PHONES

The best health and fitness apps for seniors | WhistleOut
www.whistleout.com.au/MobilePhones/Guides/best..

18 Unexpectedly Innovative Apps for Seniors in 2019

foxhillresidences.com/18-unexpectedly-innovative...

Senior Citizen Apps | 2019's Best Apps for Seniors and the ...
www.seniorliving.org/cell-phone/apps

16 Helpful Apps for Seniors
seniornet.org/blog/16-helpful-apps-for-seniors

10 Best iPhone Apps for Seniors | The Senior List
www.theseniorlist.com/cell-phones/best/iphone-apps

8 Best Senior Dating Apps (2019) - Reviews by Experts
www.datingadvice.com/apps/senior

Best Apps for Seniors - A Place for Mom

www.aplaceformom.com/blog/best-apps-for-seniors

10 Helpful Apps for Senior Citizens - Lifehack

www.lifehack.org/447838/10-helpful-apps-for.

Top 20 Apps for Senior Citizens - Sunrise Senior Living

www.sunriseseniorliving.com/blog/november-2013/.

Use These Apps to Make Android Easier for Senior Citizens

techwiser.com/android-apps-for-old-people

A List of Great Smartphone Fitness Apps for Older Adults

www.nextavenue.org/smartphone-apps-fitness

Top 6 Easiest Smartphones for Seniors in 2019 - Mobility With ...

www.mobilitywithlove.com/easiest-smartphones-for..

The 7 Best Cell Phones for Seniors in 2019 - lifewire.com

www.lifewire.com/best-cell-phones-for-senior.

Fun and Practical Tablet Apps for Seniors (Updated for 2019!)

www.multiculturalcaregiving.net/fun-and-practical-tablet..

10 Brain Training Apps for Seniors for 2019 | finder.com.au

www.finder.com.au/best-brain-training-apps-for..

Senior Fitness - Strength & Flexibility Training - Apps on ...

play.google.com/store/apps/details?id=com..

Tinder for Seniors - Senior Dating App for Singles Over 60
www.tinderforseniors.com

5 Best Senior Dating Sites (2019) - See Reviews
www.datingadvice.com/senior

8 Great Apps For Our Elders - forbes.com
www.forbes.com/.../08/28/8-great-apps-for-our-elders

Health Apps for Seniors: Tap into the Gold Mine! -- MobileSmith
www.mobilesmith.com/health_apps_for_seniors_gold.

The Top 8 Mobile Apps for Healthy, Social Seniors | Senior ...
www.seniorlifestyle.com/top-8-mobile-apps-active.

The Five Best Medical Alert Apps for Seniors | Top Ten Reviews
www.toptenreviews.com/best-medical-alert-apps

Best Android Launchers for Senior or Visually Impaired Users
www.maketecheasier.com/best-android-launchers..

GRIEF AND LOSS

Grief: Physical Symptoms, Effects on Body, Duration of Process
www.webmd.com/balance/normal-grieving-and-stages...

Grief - Wikipedia
en.wikipedia.org/wiki/Grief

**YOUTUBE: The Brain and
Grief**:https://video.search.yahoo.com/search/video?fr=mcafee&p=grief#i
d=5&vid=74ce4c24e81bfac4e6ddc965a3c2c65d&action=click

YOUTUBE: The 5 Stages of Grief:

https://video.search.yahoo.com/search/video?fr=mcafee&p=grief#id=2&vid=c5be5c61596fab0fad2b115fc160dd4e&action=view

YOUTUBE: Yoga for Grief:

https://video.search.yahoo.com/search/video?fr=mcafee&p=grief#id=3&vid=eb198a628618338639a0cfcbd88aa411&action=view

TEDTALKS: How to get from Grief to Recovery:

https://video.search.yahoo.com/search/video?fr=mcafee&p=grief#id=9&vid=d82186d53b2ebf8560c3e7515083d455&action=view

TEDTALKS: Transforming our Grief by just Showing up:

https://video.search.yahoo.com/search/video?fr=mcafee&p=grief#id=8&vid=43dcbc8d11d41bbdc00e1924c9f045e9&action=view

YOUTUBE: Guided Meditation for Loss:

https://video.search.yahoo.com/search/video?fr=mcafee&p=grief#id=17&vid=a1818e25cd7a29e9988becbf0e529a79&action=view

YOUTUBE: How you can help a friend through Grief:

https://video.search.yahoo.com/search/video?fr=mcafee&p=grief#id=18&vid=5520c3f15123dfa680b476a28cd16893&action=view

TEDTALKS: Deep Grief and Divine Ceremony:

https://video.search.yahoo.com/search/video?fr=mcafee&p=grief#id=35&vid=51bbb738e0dbe9fb479e49961a7a0754&action=view

YOUTUBE: Surviving Pet Loss Grief:

https://video.search.yahoo.com/search/video?fr=mcafee&p=grief#id=31&vid=426726348e8fbe4b6df230e181283cec&action=view

YOUTUBE: How do you help a friend through Grief?

https://video.search.yahoo.com/search/video?fr=mcafee&p=grief#id=50&vid=e3b68bc0ac15bf152c0fbcb51e1329fa&action=view

TRAVEL

Tours and Cruises for Single Seniors
www.tripsavvy.com/tours-and-cruises-for-single..

The Best Vacations for Single Senior Citizens | USA Today
traveltips.usatoday.com/vacations-single-senior...

ElderTreks
www.eldertreks.com

Senior Travel Groups: 6 Tours for Like-Minded Senior Tourists
travel-wise.com/senior-travel-groups/?all=1

What Are Senior Travel Clubs? And Should You Join One?
sixtyandme.com/what-are-senior-travel-clubs

Road Scholar
www.roadscholar.org

Small Group Tours & Travel, Big Adventures | Intrepid Travel US
www.intrepidtravel.com/us

Women Only Solo Travel
www.women-traveling.com

Group Travel Program - Group Tours | EF Go Ahead Tours
www.goaheadtours.com/groups

Why small group travel | Intrepid Travel US
www.intrepidtravel.com/.../why-small-group-travel

Gate 1 Travel
www.gate1travel.com

Trafalgar Tours - All Tours & Trips in 2019/2020 - TourRadar
www.tourradar.com/o/trafalgar

Collette Tours - All Tours & Trips in 2019/2020 - TourRadar
www.tourradar.com/o/collette-vacations

Escorted Tours - Globus® Official Site
www.globusjourneys.com

Southeast Asia Tour Packages with Airfare from the USA ...
smartours.com/southeast-asia

10 Best Southeast Asia Tours October 2019 | Easy Tours
www.easytours.travel/southeast-asia.htm

Royal Caribbean International
www.royalcaribbean.com

Carnival Cruise Line
www.carnival.com

Princess Cruises
www.princess.com

8 Best Cruise Lines for the Money
travel.usnews.com/cruises/best-cruise-lines-for-the-money

TRAVEL INSURANCE

The best 3 Travel Insurances for Seniors:
https://www.investopedia.com/articles/insurance/112616/3-best-travel-insurance-options-seniors.asp

Travel Insurance for Seniors:
https://www.allianztravelinsurance.com/travel/seniors

Senior Travel Insurance:
https://www.travelinsurancereview.net/trips/senior/

Other E-Books and Paperbacks by RLT Publishing:

Dr. T's Living Well Series:

"Overcoming Anger in Teens and Pre-Teens: A Parent's Guide"

"Overcoming Trauma and Loss in Teens and Pre-Teens: A Parent's Guide"

"Overcoming Drug and Alcohol Problems in Teens and Pre-Teens: A Parent's Guide"

"Overcoming ADHD in Teens and Pre-Teens: A Parent's Guide"

"Overcoming Anxiety in Teens and Pre-Teens: A Parent's Guide"

"Overcoming Depression in Teens and Pre-Teens: A Parent's Guide"

"Overcoming Obesity in Teens and Pre-Teens: A Parent's Guide"

"Overcoming Self-Esteem Problems in Teens and Pre-Teens: A Parent's Guide"

"Sexual Identity? Moving from Confusion to Clarity"

"A Gay Man's Guide to Love and Relationships"

"Say What? Suggestions on what to Say in almost every Difficult Situation"

"Tech Etiquette: OMG"

"Guided Imagery"

"The Traveling Parent"

Dr. T's Addiction Series:

"Validation Addiction: Please Make Me Feel Worthy"

"Addicted Nurses: Healing the Caregiver"

"Addicted Physicians: Healing the Healer"

"Addicted Pharmacists: Healing the 'Medicine Man'"

"Addicted Pilots: Flight Plan to Recovery"

"Addiction in the LGBTQ Community"

Dr. Richard L. Travis

If you learned from this book, "Senior Moments," and feel that someone else could benefit from reading it, please go back to the Amazon page where it was purchased and do a REVIEW. (If you scroll down on the purchase page you will see a place to do a customer review.)

Thank you......RLT Publishing

[OBJ]

Information about the Author

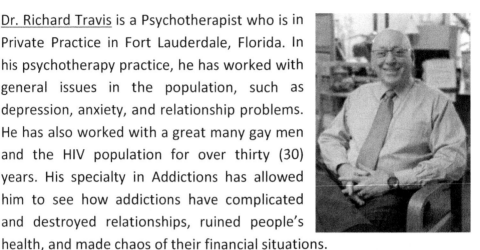

Dr. Richard Travis is a Psychotherapist who is in Private Practice in Fort Lauderdale, Florida. In his psychotherapy practice, he has worked with general issues in the population, such as depression, anxiety, and relationship problems. He has also worked with a great many gay men and the HIV population for over thirty (30) years. His specialty in Addictions has allowed him to see how addictions have complicated and destroyed relationships, ruined people's health, and made chaos of their financial situations.

He received his first master's degree at Edinboro University of Pennsylvania in Education. He received his second master's degree in Counselor Education at Florida Atlantic University in Boca Raton, Florida. He received his Doctorate in Higher Education/Counseling Psychology at Florida International University in Miami, Florida. He has Specialties in Mood Disorders, Trauma, EMDR, Hypnosis and Addictions, including State, National and International certifications in Addictions. He has worked with several people in the healthcare industry who have been in Addiction Monitoring Programs and has facilitated several groups a month with professionals being monitored by state and federal agencies.

Dr. Travis has taught classes with every age level of student in Pennsylvania, Michigan, and Florida, including teaching graduate Social Work classes at Florida International University in Miami. He has also published several articles on the website Ezinearticles.com. See more about Dr. Travis at DrRichardTravis.com

Printed in Great Britain
by Amazon

25650562R00057